# Now Playing:
# Learning World History Through Film

# Now Playing:
# Learning World History Through Film

Jonathan Perry

*University of South Florida—*

*Sarasota-Manatee*

New York   Oxford

Oxford University Press

Oxford University Press is a department of the University of Oxford.
It furthers the University's objective of excellence in research,
scholarship, and education by publishing worldwide.

Oxford    New York
Auckland    Cape Town    Dar es Salaam    Hong Kong    Karachi
Kuala Lumpur    Madrid    Melbourne    Mexico City    Nairobi
New Delhi    Shanghai    Taipei    Toronto

With offices in
Argentina    Austria    Brazil    Chile    Czech Republic    France    Greece
Guatemala    Hungary    Italy    Japan    Poland    Portugal    Singapore
South Korea    Switzerland    Thailand    Turkey    Ukraine    Vietnam

Published by Oxford University Press
198 Madison Avenue, New York, NY 10016
www.oup.com

Oxford is a registered trademark of Oxford University Press

ISBN 978-0-19-998957-7

Printing number: 9 8 7 6 5 4 3 2 1

Printed in the United States of America
on acid-free paper

# Contents

*A mi ahijado*

Patrick Brendan Joseph Sheehan

# Introduction

Speaking about his experiences in writing the screenplay for *Danton* (1983), Jean-Claude Carrière (the author of two of the screenplays profiled in this book) observed that film is the only medium available for 'recreating history'. Because we cannot ourselves live in the past or view it for ourselves, he suggests, the filmmaker can transport an audience back in time, at least to some extent. He concedes that *Danton*, like any other artistic product, also reflects its own time and that as a result the context of Europe, and specifically of Poland, in the early 1980s must be taken into account in the film's interpretation today.

Furthermore, Carrière commented on the particular challenge he faced in reconstructing Danton's final speech to his accusers before being sentenced to death. As there is no surviving transcript of that speech, Carrière was obliged to craft a speech 'that should have been said' on this occasion. Whether consciously or not, he was in this admission echoing precisely what Thucydides had claimed for his own speeches, set during the unfolding Peloponnesian War: 'Some I heard myself, others I got from various places; it was in all cases difficult to carry them word for word in one's memory, so my habit has been to make the speakers say what was in my opinion demanded of them by the various occasions—of course, adhering as closely as possible to the general sense of what they really said' (Thucydides' *History of the Peloponnesian War*, I.22).

The main argument of this book is that an in-depth study of certain key films, set at formative moments in the history of world civilization, can help flesh out the details offered in a textbook treatment. The enormous power of film to shape perceptions of the past normally makes professors recoil in horror; it can be very annoying for a professor to explain, seemingly for the millionth time, that something a student has seen in a film and vaguely recalls for an examination is not 'historically accurate'. On the other hand, if handled with due caution, film can enhance the student's learning experience and lavish specific images, color, and sound upon elements that might seem lifeless on the textbook page.

Selecting the 32 films to be incorporated into this book, which covers the entire span of human history from its beginnings to the present, has been especially challenging. However, certain principles have guided the selection process. The first goal was specifically to match the selections to the chapters in the remarkably thorough and well-designed textbook *Patterns of World History*. Even though it proved impossible to find a film to match each chapter in the text, virtually every chapter in *Patterns* can now be experienced alongside one or at the most two films that touch on topics raised within it.

Moreover, the attempt was made to include directors from as many different national backgrounds as possible. My hope is that students will come to appreciate the richness and profundity of contemporary global cinema and seek out more examples of it. Even more importantly, it can be fascinating to watch a modern person grappling with the legacy of his or her own national past in a historical film. Accordingly, Japanese history may best be appreciated by a Japanese director, Malian history by a Malian, Argentinian by an Argentinian, Australian by an Australian, etc. To paraphrase the novelist William Faulkner, who applied this concept to his own vision of the southern United States, the past is never truly dead, nor is it even past.

Nevertheless, in spite of their geographical and chronological span, there are at least three themes that have consistently been revisited by several films. A favorite subject among many directors throughout the twentieth and twenty-first centuries concerns the dangers of religious faith, usually described as hypersensitive, bullying, and violent, emphasizing toleration as a calm, collected, but perhaps also naïve antidote to religious bigotry. While explaining the views of various religious figures, and often the founders of the great world religions, they also make an effective—and timely—case for tolerating and accepting differences of opinion.

Cross-cultural encounter is always a central component in a course on world history, and film has pointed up the ironies, complexities, and most often the violence inherent to these encounters. Several of the films profiled here have recognized the intensely dramatic potential of human interaction, especially when the cultures involved seem so utterly incongruous at first appearance. Some of the more sophisticated films, however, have also suggested that the impact can work in dynamic and exciting ways, in which both the aggressor and the victim can be fundamentally transformed and even fused into a new civilization.

A third theme, and especially one that has emerged in response to the seemingly never-ending warfare of the twentieth, and now the twenty-first, centuries, addresses the horrors that have characterized all wars in human history. Filmmakers have often focused on those who suffer in war, and sympathy is sometimes elicited for one's enemies by means of a long scream or a piece of music played for the victims of both sides of a conflict. Perhaps it is only when we realize that people on the 'other' side of warfare also bleed when pricked that peace can be imagined.

# *Troy*

## Film Data

Year: 2004
Director: Wolfgang Petersen
Screenplay: David Benioff
Music: James Horner
Production Design: Nigel Phelps
Length: 162 minutes
Rating: R

## Connection to *Patterns of World History* & *Patterns of World History, Brief Edition*

Chapter 2: *Agrarian–Urban Centers of the Middle East and Eastern Mediterranean*

## Preview

*Troy* bears very little resemblance to Homer's *Iliad*, and it is by no means a reliable introduction to the events chronicled in this Ur-text of Greek civilization. Nevertheless, the film is still worth viewing, particularly in respect to its *mise-en-scène*—as Western powers were again engaged in war in western Asia in the early twenty-first century—and to its director's fundamental vision of war's realities.

The *Iliad* opens with Achilles' wrath over the confiscation of his 'prize' Briseis by the Greeks' overlord Agamemnon, and it concludes with the abeyance of Achilles' wrath, when he bows to King Priam's plea to reclaim the body of his son Hector. The epic addresses only the final year—and not even the entirety of that year—in the 10-year-long struggle of the Greeks to reclaim Helen from the Trojans. This film, by contrast, attempts to cover the entirety of the war, from its origins to its conclusion by means of the Trojan horse. Gratuitous errors mar the film as a whole, but it preserves some of Homer's original intentions. These may have been to demonstrate the need to sympathize with one's enemies and to acknowledge that right and humanity may be on the other side as well as on one's own.

The film preserves some of the central episodes of the *Iliad*, developing the contrast between Achilles, who is weary with blustering commanders and the futility of war, and Hector, who is equally noble and equally driven by his love for a woman. In this regard, the film is far less brave than Oliver Stone's *Alexander*, which was also released in 2004 and unapologetically underscored Alexander's bisexual behavior and perhaps his identity as well. In Petersen's *Troy*, Patroclus is merely Achilles' 'cousin', and not his companion and lover. A safely heterosexual Achilles in this context may tell us more about contemporary attitudes toward sexuality than anything Homer's audience would have understood.

In interviews about the film, the German Petersen has referred to another German, the remarkable amateur archaeologist Heinrich Schliemann who, Homer in hand, had attempted to find the Troy of the *Iliad* in the late nineteenth century. Despite the sneers and dismissive attitudes of ancient historians, Schliemann—with the help of an underappreciated British enthusiast called Frank Calvert—found remnants of what could have been an actual Troy in modern northwestern Turkey. When he decided to film the Trojan War story, Petersen similarly turned to existing records, but he also employed his imagination for a vaguely 'Mycenaean' production design. Some elements in the royal palaces of Mycenae and Troy recall elements of actual Bronze Age archaeology, but others were imported from widely varying contexts, such as ancient Egypt, Mesopotamia, and Persia. Intrigued by the challenge of resurrecting the world of 1250 BCE, he combined these design elements into enormous sets, had hundreds of soldiers from the Bulgarian and Mexican armies trained in the 'battle techniques' of the period, and employed new computer-generated imaging (CGI) technology to flesh out the details.

Having shot some of the film in Malta, Petersen hoped to shoot the remainder on Morocco's Atlantic coast. However, the turmoil that came to shake the Middle East, accelerated by the invasion of Iraq in early 2003, necessitated a change of venue. Petersen moved production to Mexico's Baja California and weathered a hurricane and other natural and manmade disasters. Thus, modern warfare actually shaped the making of this film, and the present may never have been far removed from Petersen's original conception. Petersen observed how difficult it was for his actors and the extras to bear up under brutal sunshine, heat, and constantly pouring sweat, observing, 'Our battles are not glorious.'

Perhaps the theme of this film is that, regardless of how long one's name lives on in history books and in epic poetry, war is never a glorious exercise. Petersen had first come to international attention for his searing portrait of German sailors trapped in a submarine during World War II in 1981's *Das Boot* (*The Boat*). By sharing the suffering of 'the enemy', one can experience the indignities and the horrors of war, on all sides of a conflict. Thus, while the gods are conspicuously absent from Petersen's *Troy*, larger themes of war and its true nature abound in the piece.

## Recommended Scenes

➤ Hector discovers that his brother Paris has lured Helen away from her husband Menelaus, and Menelaus offers his brother Agamemnon a perfect pretext for a war on Troy, 00:16:20 through 00:21:15.
➤ While the image was pared down from its original conception, a CGI shot of the flotilla of Greek ships and their initial landing on Troy's beaches is offered between 00:35:48 and 00:44:31.
➤ Achilles confronts the warmonger Agamemnon over his confiscation of Briseis, 00:53:42 through 00:56:34.
➤ Hector kills Patroclus, who is wearing Achilles' armor, and Hector prepares for the final conflict by comforting his wife Andromache and their infant Astyanax, 01:43:18 through 01:50:35.
➤ The highlight of the film is the final duel between Hector (played by Eric Bana) and Brad Pitt's Achilles, 01:57:37 through 02:03:30. The battle is effectively choreographed and is completely the work of the actors themselves—with the accentuated sound of swords whizzing through the air.
➤ A regal Peter O'Toole, playing Priam, comes to Achilles' tent to beg for Hector's body, 02:05:20 through 02:11:55. Achilles grieves over the corpse of his great enemy as well.

## Discussion Questions

1.  Does the film bear out its director's observation that there is nothing 'glorious' about war?

2.  What contemporary allusions may *Troy* have been making to the world of 2004?

3.  How does the film reinforce the concept of respect for one's enemies?

## Further Reading and Viewing

Petersen's *Das Boot* (1981) introduces similarly ambiguous themes of war and its justification, as does his *In the Line of Fire* (1993), a reflection on presidential security told through the weary eyes of a US Secret Service officer.

The best analyses of the film can be found in Martin M. Winkler's edited volume *Troy: From Homer's Iliad to Hollywood Epic* (Blackwell Publishers, 2007). Particularly remarkable in this book are the essays by J. Lesley Fitton, 'Troy and the Role of the Historical Advisor', pp. 99–106 (which asks whether a historical advisor would have made any difference in the end result), and, in delightfully ironic mode, Jon Solomon's 'Viewing *Troy*: Authenticity, Criticism, and Interpretation', pp. 85–98.

# *The Mahabharata*

## Film Data

Year: 1989
Director: Peter Brook
Screenplay: Jean-Claude Carrière
Length: 170 minutes
Rating: No rating

## Connection to *Patterns of World History* & *Patterns of World History, Brief Edition*

Chapter 3: *Shifting Agrarian Centers in India*

## Preview

*The Mahabharata* was the result of a unique multinational collaboration, focusing renewed attention on one of the foundational epics of Indian culture. The acclaimed British theater director Peter Brook reached out to the French scriptwriter Jean-Claude Carrière, who had come to international attention through his screenplay for *Danton* (1983), offering him the chance to dramatize the 100,000-line *Mahabharata* for television. Given the enormous size of the poem, Carrière was forced to shorten and condense the epic's main elements into an intelligible format, and, from its first installments, the miniseries was welcomed as a bold and imaginative attempt to modernize one of the world's most ancient documents. Originally spread over 10 hours in its original release in 1989, *The Mahabharata* is now available in a 3-hour condensed version for a 2008 DVD.

As conceived by Brook and Carrière, the *Mahabharata* was a central document of human history and not merely the history of South Asia. In respect to this notion, they deliberately chose a multi-ethnic cast, with only one Indian actor, portraying the princess Draupadi. For a few examples, Arjuna was performed by an Italian actor, Bhima by a Senegalese, and the remaining roles were played by actors from Indonesia, Japan, and France, among many other nations. Intended to have universal appeal, *The Mahabharata*, like the *Iliad*, focuses upon a war between ruling families, and, again like the *Iliad*, it retains the sense of its original oral transmission. The film preserves the flavor of an oral poem that is eventually written down by means of a clever framing device. At the beginning of the film, a boy approaches a poet, who begins to tell his story with Ganesha the scribe taking dictation. At the conclusion, Ganesha hands the complete written *Mahabharata* to the boy, and he is now the owner, like the viewer, of a compelling 'story of mankind'.

While the universal appeal and relevance of the poem to the modern day is repeatedly underscored in the film, its original source material was rooted in a particular historical context. Because it centers on the struggles between kings and princes, the *Mahabharata* can be read to reflect the ideological components of rulership in ancient India. At its center is a power struggle between the descendants of two brothers, culminating in a comprehensive war that ends in the victory of one branch of the family over the other. Elements of philosophy, religion, and moral behavior appear throughout the poem, and the concepts of *dharma* (natural law, correct behavior) and chaos are introduced by Krishna, the wise sage who appears at critical moments to explain the wider application of what seems a simple battle narrative. The unique contributions of Indian culture to philosophy and religion find their beginning in the Vedic tales, and this film suggests that they remain useful in today's global culture.

## Recommended Scenes

➢ The poet describes the origins of the main characters of the story, between 00:05:22 and 00:15:18. A king surrenders power to his blind brother and has five sons (the Pandava) by his queen Kunti. The queen has already had a son, Karna, born to the sun-god, but she abandoned him to be raised by a 'driver'. The blind king and his blindfolded queen have produced 100 sons of their own, and the conflict among these cousins will result in open war.

➢ The five brothers are collectively married to the beautiful princess Draupadi, 00:24:35 through 00:34:06. In Indian tradition, she is equated to the palm holding together the hand's five fingers.

➢ After the eldest of the five brothers loses his inheritance, his brothers, and their wife in a game of dice, the Pandava are forced into exile. A war is predicted, and the philosophy of detachment from existence is explored, 00:52:18 through 00:56:27.

> ➢ Arjuna, the most skillful warrior among the brothers, acquires the ultimate weapon from Shiva and prepares for conflict with his cousins. However, he worries about the prospect of bringing war against his own family and confers with Krishna about the meaning of the conflict, 01:35:35 through 01:48:10.

> ➢ The battle begins, and Arjuna engages in single combat with Karna, who is revealed to be his lost half-brother, 02:25:08 through 02:30:09.

> ➢ Ganesha hands the completed *Mahabharata* to the boy, who leaves the scene carrying a lengthy manuscript, 02:44:44 through 02:48:10.

## Discussion Questions

1. What scenes can be paralleled with the epics of other ancient peoples, particularly the Jewish scriptures and Homeric literature?

2. Was the *Mahabharata* concerned with moral behavior?

3. How does the epic comment on the 'ideology of rulership' in ancient India?

## Further Reading and Viewing

The 2008 DVD release of the film contains an extensive 'making-of' documentary explaining the unique casting choices and ultimate success of the television project. The *Mahabharata* is available in many up-to-date translations, with extensive notes, the most useful of which is probably the abridged Penguin edition (2009). Even this translation is, however, 912 pages in length.

# *Confucius*

## Film Data

Year: 2010
Director: Hu Mei
Music: Zhao Jiping
Length: 125 minutes
Rating: No rating

## Connection to *Patterns of World History* & *Patterns of World History, Brief Edition*

Chapter 4: *Agrarian Centers and the Mandate of Heaven in Ancient China*

Chapter 9: *China: Imperial Unification and Perfecting the Moral Order*

## Preview

This film is a conventional 'bio-pic' of the founder of one of the world's great religions, and it reflects many of the difficulties inherent to this cinematic genre. The details of Confucius' life are murky and disordered, especially given the chaos surrounding the declining Zhou period and specifically in the 490s and 480s BCE. The name 'Confucius' was, of course, a Western rendering of his original name, Kong Qiu, and the film draws attention to the impact of politics and interstate conflict throughout Kong's career. Nevertheless, it was particularly challenging to dramatize Kong's philosophical insights within a biographical framework, and, as we shall see with *Siddhartha* (1972), this challenge was not unique to the story of Confucianism. While the narrative is bogged down in extraneous details and has a ponderous feel, Zhao Jiping's music is one of the film's best elements, contributing to the emotional impact of the story by incorporating both Western and Chinese themes.

The hand of governmental funding and control in modern Chinese cinema must also be acknowledged in this context. The film repeatedly draws attention to the need for unity among the various warring states, and, while it underscores Kong's love for his own kingdom of Lu, it suggests that Confucianism could provide the basis for national unity.

*Confucius* also stresses Kong's background, as a commoner who was effectively shut out of power by the three noble clans of Lu. Despite his wise advice to the King of Lu, Kong is eventually driven out and forced to wander among the other states, due to the resentment of this traditional aristocracy. The aristocrats are here depicted as warmongers and incompetent managers who persist in barbaric customs long after Kong has demonstrated a more civilized way of life.

Throughout the film, Kong is depicted as a calm, wise, and universally respected presence whose advice should be followed. He appears most serene and comfortable when speaking with his students, whether young men or, in an interesting twist on traditional notions, the beautiful Queen Consort (a former courtesan) of a neighboring kingdom. Despite the resistance of warring aristocrats, Kong advocates a new approach to government, in which respect for the weak, poor, and defenseless will form the basis for civil society. To what extent this philosophy was meant to be applied outside the ruling class is left unclear in the film as, perhaps, it was in history.

## Recommended Scenes

➤ In an effective opening, contrasting the civilized attitudes of Kong Qiu with the barbarity of the Ji family, 'burial slaves' are ritually slaughtered and buried with a member of the Ji clan, 00:04:11 through 00:10:03.

➤ Rising to become the principal advisor to the King of Lu, Kong helps the king to avoid war with the neighboring kingdom of Qi and defends him against rebel attack, 00:40:23 through 00:55:28.

➤ Despite his services to Lu, Kong is outmaneuvered by the three noble families, dismissed from his office, and, literally, forced into the wilderness. He is, however, accompanied by his students and begins his wanderings in 497 BCE.

➤ Kong is invited to the court of the beautiful and intellectually curious Queen of Wei, but she is assassinated in the midst of the interstate struggles plaguing China in the period, 01:14:17 through 01:29:20.

➤ The King of Qi attacks Lu, and the noble families begin to realize what they have lost by sending Kong away. Nevertheless, Kong continues to instruct his students, maintaining a strict asceticism as they nearly starve and attempt to keep up their spirits with music and conversation, 01:38:05 through 01:46:07.

> ➤ Kong agrees to return to Lu but insists that he will only teach and not be involved in politics. His return (in 484 BCE) is described, and, between 01:55:40 and 02:01:42, he is pictured as an old man among his books, still cheerfully and wisely instructing his disciples until his death 5 years later.

## Discussion Questions

1.    What, according to the film, constitute the principles of effective government in Confucianism?

2.    How does Kong contrast civilized and barbaric behavior throughout his life?

3.    How does the film address the theme of unification, in the midst of the interstate warfare of the period?

## Further Reading and Viewing

A brief narrative of Confucius' life is available in Jonathan Clements' *Confucius: A Biography* (Sutton Publishing, 2004), and there is an accessible translation of Confucius' *Analects* by Edward Slingerland (Hackett Publishing, 2003).

# *Alexander*

## Film Data

Year: 2004
Director: Oliver Stone
Screenplay: Oliver Stone, Christopher Kyle, and Laeta Kalogridis
Historical Consultant: Robin Lane Fox
Music: Vangelis
Length: 175 minutes
Rating: R

## Connection to *Patterns of World History* & *Patterns of World History, Brief Edition*

Chapter 7: *Persia, Greece, and Rome*

## Preview

Despite being an element of the wavelet of ancient historical films produced in the wake of *Gladiator* (2000), Oliver Stone's film may have fallen, as Jon Solomon has commented, 'into the category of films that are condemned because of unfortunate timing.' The micro-timing of its US release—immediately after the reelection of President George W. Bush in November 2004—was certainly a factor in its reception by the American public. Stone has repeatedly 'revisited' *Alexander*, attempting to discover why 'We did four times the business outside America than we did in America', according to a 2005 interview for *The Times* (UK).

This particular box-office failure has widely been attributed to the oblique references to Alexander's bisexuality—and to the results of the US elections, in which 11 states had voted to ban same-sex marriage as part of a strategy that was believed to enhance turnout for the President. Stone observed, in the 2005 interview, 'Once "Alexander the Gay" came out—that was the headline [in *The New York Post*], which was very cheesy—that killed it. You don't combine homosexuality or bisexuality with military men in America'. In an extended interview in *Cinéaste* in March 2005, Stone insisted that the film's depiction of Alexander's relationship with Hephaestion was 'nothing unusual' for the period and that 'We adhered to the historical record of Alexander as faithfully as we could'. He added that, while some were pruriently caught up in the depiction of same-sex sexual encounters, he was more interested in Hephaestion as Alexander's 'soul mate'. With great sensitivity and emotional sophistication, Stone pointed to the fact of Alexander's mammoth grief at the death of his lover: 'He built a funeral pyre five stories high—I wish I could have filmed that!—and I believe he was so consumed with grief that he never recovered'.

Although Alexander's emotional attachments were always of greater interest to Stone than his subject's sexual nature, the controversy has overshadowed the real achievements of this film in terms of its visual and musical language, its clever narrative techniques, and its faithfulness to historical sources. Recalling some of the best elements of his famous score for *Chariots of Fire* (1982), Vangelis (a native of modern Thessaly and thus a near-neighbor, in some respects, to the Macedonians) crafted pulsating, variegated music to enhance the dramatic intensity of the film.

Particularly in the battle scenes, Stone employed unusual camera angles, as when an eagle literally provides a bird's-eye view of the armies at Gaugamela, and he moved quickly from one quadrant of the battle to another to capture the fog (or the flying sand) of war. The highlight of the film is probably the sequence detailing his confrontation with Porus in India, which may recall Stone's own experience as a soldier in the Vietnam conflict and his previous films like *Platoon* (1986) and *Born on the Fourth of July* (1989). The sequence begins with a shaking camera as elephants thunder through the jungle and ends with a red filter over the scene to demonstrate Alexander's field of vision after being wounded. This segment also features what may be the film's iconic moment, a slow-motion rearing of the horse Bucephalus carrying Alexander confronting a rearing elephant carrying Porus. The image was surely borrowed from the famous 'Elephant Medallions', which show Indians on elephants launching spears on Alexander and his rearing horse. (For analysis of these medallions, see especially Frank L. Holt's *Alexander the Great and the Mystery of the Elephant Medallions* (University of California Press, 2003).)

Some have criticized the narrative structure of the film, which is framed as the spoken memories of Ptolemy recalling the events of Alexander's life after 40 years. This must have been due to the influence of Robin Lane Fox, Stone's historical consultant and author of a definitive 1973 biography,  since Ptolemy did write a memoir that was used, at least by Arrian in the second century CE. The narrative is not structured as a simple birth-to-death account but rather is composed of a general narrative line with impressively designed flashbacks.

For one example, the narrative of Cleitus' murder by Alexander triggers a memory of the assassination of Philip II. The appropriateness of this connection is underscored by Cleitus' briefly morphing into Philip in the midst of his confrontation with Alexander. Having murdered Cleitus, as a sort of father-figure and vestige of old-fashioned Macedonian values, Alexander remembers the assassination of Philip and wonders whether he could be held responsible for that murder, too. The connection of Cleitus and Philip was not Stone's or Lane Fox's invention; it is borrowed directly from Arrian, 4.8-9.

The overall theme of the film is extremely well chosen and apposite for the first decade of the twenty-first century. Alexander's vision of a blended culture, connecting Greeks and non-Greeks, grows as he moves further into the East. In a series of encounters with his dubious Macedonian generals, Alexander sketches out this vision, observing that 'We're in new worlds' and asking Cassander what makes him and the other Greeks 'so much better' than the disparate peoples they have conquered. In one of the script's most remarkable lines, Alexander condemns Cassander's 'contempt for a world far older than ours', and twenty-first-century audiences might reasonably have connected Alexander's experiences in Mesopotamia with the ongoing US-led war in Iraq. Ptolemy eventually concludes that 'the dreamers exhaust us' with their impossible dreams, but the notions of world unity and learning from other cultures might still seem worthy dreams.

## Recommended Scenes

➢ NB: References to time counters should be connected to the 'Theatrical Release' DVD version and not to the 'Director's Cut' or 'The Final Cut' (released in 2007).

➢ Olympias (convincingly and ferociously played by Angelina Jolie) instills the legend of Achilles in her son Alexander, and her hatred for Philip is explained between 00:10:15 and 00:12:45.

➢ Borrowing directly from Plutarch's *Life of Alexander*, Chapter 6, Alexander tames the wild horse Bucephalus to the delight of his father, 00:17:24 through 00:22:22.

➢ Like Robert Rossen's *Alexander the Great* (1956), the film depicts the actions and words associated with Philip's marriage to Eurydice/Cleopatra, 00:30:10 through 00:35:36.

➢ An extraordinary recreation of the Battle of Gaugamela is presented between 00:37:48 and 01:02:02.

➤ Although some details are transposed from the ancient sources and misconstrued, a female member of Darius' family is treated respectfully and chivalrously by the conqueror Alexander, 01:10:15 through 01:21:47.

➤ [The remaining scenes are found on the second disc, with times beginning again:]

➤ Alexander is intrigued by the dancing princess Roxane and confronts his Macedonian generals over his decision to marry her, 00:00:10 through 00:08:07.

➤ The Pages' Conspiracy is moved from its proper chronological place and tied to the liquidation of Philotas and his father Parmenio, 00:16:46 through 00:27:00.

➤ In the midst of a drunken dinner party Cleitus verbally assaults Alexander and Alexander spears him, 00:31:20 through 00:35:34.

➤ The murder of Cleitus triggers Alexander's memories of Philip's assassination—and Olympias' complicity in it, between 00:39:15 and 00:48:45.

➤ Alexander's battle with Porus is depicted (in a jungle rather than at the Hydaspes)—and his most serious wound is transposed to this battle, 00:56:10 through 01:07:10.

➤ After Hephaestion's death, Alexander falls into a tailspin, which may or may not have been accentuated by poison. After his death, the 'successors' literally fight over his body in a particularly appropriate scene, 01:18:04 through 01:23:55.

## Discussion Questions

1.    How do the deeds and images of Philip continue to haunt his son's life?

2.    How does Stone characterize the relationship between Alexander and Hephaestion?

3.    Is Alexander articulating a realistic, realizable goal of East–West unity?

## Further Reading and Viewing

Oliver Stone released three separate and distinct DVD versions of *Alexander*, as he continually 'revisited' the film and its commercial failure, but the most effective, for the purposes of a historian, is the 'Theatrical Release' version. This two-disc set contains an audio commentary track by Stone and Robin Lane Fox, and Fox's experiences as a historical advisor (who was permitted to be an extra on horseback at the recreation of Gaugamela) are interlaced with the scenes in a lively style.

Paul Cartledge's *The Alexander the Great: The Hunt for a New Past* (New York: Vintage Books, 2004) is an effective introduction to the study of Alexander, and a full scholarly analysis, through a series of essays, was published in P. Cartledge and F.R. Greenland (eds.), *Responses to Oliver Stone's Alexander: Film, History, and Cultural Studies* (Madison: University of Wisconsin Press, 2010). The most interesting papers in this set are probably the editors' introduction (pp. 3–12) and Oliver Stone's response (pp. 337–351), which proves his academic engagement with the topic and openness to criticism from professional ancient historians.

Appreciative commentaries on *Alexander*—and on its use by historians and students of history—can be found in Jon Solomon's 'Model of a Lesser God', *Arion* 13 (Spring–Summer 2005), pp. 149–160, and in Angelos Chaniotis' 'Making Alexander Fit for the Twenty-First Century: Oliver Stone's *Alexander*', in I. Berti and M. García Morcillo (eds.), *Hellas on Screen: Cinematic Receptions of Ancient History, Literature and Myth* (Stuttgart: Franz Steiner Verlag, 2008), pp. 185–201.

# *Agora*

## Film Data

Year: 2009
Director: Alejandro Amenábar
Writers: Alejandro Amenábar and Mateo Gil
Historical Advisors: Elisa Garrido and Justin Pollard
Length: 125 minutes
Rating: R

## Connection to *Patterns of World History* & *Patterns of World History, Brief Edition*

Chapter 7: *Persia, Greece, and Rome*

## Preview

*Agora* centers upon the circumstances leading to the murder of Hypatia, a philosopher, mathematician, and teacher, by a Christian mob in Alexandria (Egypt) in 415 CE. Born around 360 CE and instructed by her father Theon, a mathematician and last librarian of the famous Library at Alexandria, Hypatia directed the Platonic school in the city, teaching students who were of mixed religious commitments but, presumably, all men. The few sources that mention her agree that she was abducted, stripped of her clothes, and stoned to death with roof tiles by a deranged group of Christians, but the precise sequence of events that led to this atrocity has always been controversial. Because all of these sources were composed by Christians—with the exception of her own correspondence with a former student, the Bishop Synesius of Cyrene—the lynching of Hypatia may be interpreted as an instance of fanaticism attempting to destroy reason or as the elimination of a dangerous pagan influence in the midst of a Christianizing Egypt.

The latter approach has, unfortunately, been more common, given Christian influence—and misogyny—in Western societies and the installation of her main opponent, Bishop Cyril of Alexandria, as one of the 'Fathers of the Church'. Hypatia was even depicted as a wicked temptress in the 1853 novel *Hypatia, or New Foes with an Old Face* by Charles Kingsley (exponent of 'muscular Christianity' in Victorian Britain). A young Spanish filmmaker believed that the story of Hypatia deserved an updated and more sympathetic treatment for a new millennium, and his original idea was to include her story among those who had used reason to advance the cause of science, particularly in respect to astronomy. However, Amenábar soon came to realize that the story of Hypatia could stand alone and still speak to the concerns of Western societies in the early twenty-first century.

Deciding to recount her tale in the English language and commissioning mostly English-speaking actors for the main roles, Amenábar meticulously recreated some of the physical appearance of Alexandria in the late fourth and early fifth centuries CE, while also employing extremely innovative camera techniques and wide-angle shots to tell his story visually. He claimed that he developed his production design, from costumes to hairstyles to the casting of extras, from the famous Fayyum portraits, and he used 3-D digital storyboards and computer graphics to sketch out the main elements of the film. Most interestingly, however, he periodically pulls the camera dramatically away from the action on the ground and focuses upon the stars or upon the planet Earth moving in space. The film also offers several overhead shots of crowds moving quickly, suggesting how minuscule the actions of people might look to any of the 'gods' who are being invoked at the moment.

*Agora* can be used to illustrate one of the most significant transitional moments in Western civilization, when non-Christian intellectuals were forced to convert to the new faith or were shunted aside if they refused. While some of the scientific speculation may be inappropriate—it is unlikely, for instance, that Hypatia formulated the concept of elliptical planetary orbits, some 1,200 years before Kepler—the overall themes of the film are also of critical importance in today's world.

Determined to celebrate the 'heroism of those who use reason', the director risked offending religious adherents of all types, from Christians to Jews to Muslims. Conflicts over the proper place of religious expression in secular Western Europe constantly arise in our own time, and issues of gender and education sometimes intersect with these. France's ban on the *niqab* and other overt forms of religious identity in the public 'forum' come to mind, but one might also recall the Al Qaeda-inspired bombing of Madrid's central train station in 2004. *Agora* may be suggesting that religion simply provides the excuse for episodes of horrific violence and that scientific progress can be made only when religious dogma is not allowed to interfere.

## Recommended Scenes

➢ Captions establish the setting of the film, Alexandria in 391 CE, and a cosmic view of our planet, with the African continent filling most of the frame, is shown. In her school, Hypatia describes the Ptolemaic system of planetary motion (around the Earth, with the Earth remaining stationary) and his preference for 'perfect' circles, 00:00:40 through 00:03:43.

➢ Outraged by the growing numbers of Christian slaves in his household, Hypatia's father Theon beats Davus, and Hypatia tends to his wounds. Clearly in love with his mistress, Davus makes a model of the Ptolemaic system and explains the epicycle theory to the other students, 00:09:10 through 00:15:20.

➢ A violent riot directed by the priest of Serapis against Christians backfires, and the 'pagans' are besieged in their temple, which currently houses the remains of the Library, between 00:28:13 and 00:35:48.

➢ Negotiations allow the pagans to evacuate the Serapeum, but Hypatia is determined to save as many scrolls from the library as possible before the Christian mob comes pouring into the precinct. The Christians gleefully turn over the library's shelves and rip apart and burn what they consider 'pagan filth', 00:46:57 through 00:55:06.

➢ Another wonderful overhead shot introduces Alexandria's harbor, and many years pass (actually over 25, but Rachel Weisz, playing Hypatia, appears not to have aged). Cyril is now installed as the city's bishop, and he advocates violence against Alexandrian Jews, 00:58:50 through 01:03:35.

➢ Reprisals against this violence by Jews result in even more violence in the street, and Hypatia watches in horror as her fellow citizens destroy each other. Here again, the planetary view is given, and the screams of those killed in the violence echo into space, 01:14:02 through 01:20:03.

➢ Cyril quotes from the New Testament book I Timothy to the effect that a woman should not be suffered to instruct men, and then demands to know whether Orestes, newly installed as the city's prefect, agrees with the Bible on this point. Orestes is a former student of Hypatia and is still in love with her, even after she rejected his overtures, and so he refuses to commit himself. The monk Ammonius throws a stone at Orestes, and the targeting of Hypatia by Cyril and his followers is becoming ever more clear, 01:29:01through 01:39:35.

➢ In an extremely effective dénouement, Hypatia is confronted with the demand to submit to a public baptism and, after her refusal, is captured by Christians, stripped, and abused. Her former slave Davus suffocates her so that she can avoid the pain of stoning, and then the camera pulls back to heaven's view of this moment, between 01:47:32 and 01:59:33.

## Discussion Questions

1.     How does the camera movement in the film enhance the plot?

2.     What role does the astronomical plot play in the film?

3.     Is the film anti-Christian? Does it condemn fanaticism of all types?

## Further Reading and Viewing

Due in part to the controversy surrounding it and some attacks on it by Christian groups, *Agora* was not widely released in the United States. However, it earned favorable reviews in some quarters, and among the best is Susan Jacoby's article, 'Reason is the star of *Agora*', http://newsweek.washingtonpost.com/onfaith/spirited_atheist/2010/06/agora_a_rare_movie_with_reason_as_its_star.html. A scholarly treatment of Hypatia can be found in Maria Dzielska's *Hypatia of Alexandria* (Harvard University Press, 1995).

# *Siddhartha*

## Film Data

Year: 1972
Director: Conrad Rooks
Based on the novel by Hermann Hesse (in 1922)
Music: Hemant Kumar
Cinematography: Sven Nykvist
Length: 85 minutes
Rating: R

## Connection to *Patterns of World History* & *Patterns of World History, Brief Edition*

Chapter 8: *Empires and Visionaries in India*

## Preview

Like *Confucius* (2010), this film is a 'bio-pic' of the founder of one of the world's great religions, though made in a less conventional mode and adapted from a classic novel of the early twentieth century. The American Conrad Rooks, after an adolescence characterized by—he later admitted—expulsion from schools and experimentation with drugs and alcohol, came upon Hermann Hesse's novel about the origins of Buddhism in the life of Siddhartha Gautama in fifth-century BCE India. Captivated by the story's elements of spiritual quest and fulfillment, and a member of America's 'Brahmin' class himself as the son of a prominent business tycoon, Rooks began contemplating its cinematic potential.

Indians were suspicious of Westerners attempting to film historical subjects in their country, and, in the early 1970s, many were still resentful of a 1968 documentary made by Louis Malle that had seemed dismissive of Indian culture. However, Rooks overcame their objections and—due in great measure to his friendships with Indira Gandhi, the Maharajah of Bharatpur, and, most significantly, the Kapoors, the leading family of Indian film—he received permission to film in several holy sites within India. The talents of Shashi Kapoor, who played the title role and would also be featured in a series of Merchant–Ivory films like

*Shakespeare Wallah* (1965) and *Heat and Dust* (1983), are particularly noteworthy. However, the principal achievements in the film can be found in the lush cinematography of Sven Nykvist, who had been associated with many of Ingmar Bergman's most acclaimed projects.

The film's script is hampered by the limits of the biographical genre, and the framework of a bio-pic was not an ideal vehicle through which to convey complex philosophical concepts. *Siddhartha* draws frequent—and probably too repetitive—attention to the image of the river, which 'always returns' like everything else in life. As Rooks has commented in a recent interview, the message of his film was probably 'the opposite of a Hollywood message', but it was a critical success. While one might have expected a psychedelic, late-1960s countercultural vibe, given its creator and its immediate context, the film's style is sedate and it is beautifully shot, if not terribly profound in its ideas.

## Recommended Scenes

➤ Tired of the sameness of his life among the Brahmin elite, Siddhartha goes on a quest for spiritual fulfillment with his friend Govinda, 00:04:32 through 00:09:42.

➤ After accepting a series of gurus and finding their philosophy wanting, Siddhartha sets out again, encountering the ferryman Vasudeva, who comments that he has learned 'from the river that everything returns'. Siddhartha encounters the beautiful courtesan Kamala, whom he takes as his guru of '*kama*', sexual fulfillment, 00:25:00 through 00:32:44.

➤ Having experienced both sexual pleasure and professional success, Siddhartha is dissatisfied and sets out on another journey. Encountering Vasudeva a second time, he asks to become the ferryman's apprentice, 00:49:13 through 01:01:30.

➤ After he has aged and grown in wisdom and experience, Siddhartha takes over the boat from Vasudeva, who sails away reminding him—again—that, like the river, everything returns. Govinda returns and agrees to stay with Siddhartha, stop searching for happiness, and find peace at the river, 01:13:10 through 01:20:40.

## Discussion Questions

1.    What drives Siddhartha in his quest for spiritual fulfillment?

2.    What does the river teach Vasudeva and Siddhartha?

3.    How does the film address the concepts of detachment and *nirvana*?

## Further Reading and Viewing

The 2002 DVD release of the film contains an extended interview with Conrad Rooks in which he describes his encounters with the Beat poets and with Hesse's novel in 1950s Greenwich Village. A guide to the film and a biographical treatment of Rooks, Nykvist, and the film's lead actors may be found online at http://cdn.shopify.com/s/files/1/0150/7896/files/SiddharthaPK.pdf?1009.

Hermann Hesse's novel is available in many English translations, and there is a new biography of the novelist by Gunnar Decker entitled *Hesse: Der Wanderer und sein Schatten* [*Hesse: The Wanderer and his Shadow*] (Munich: Hanser, 2012).

# *The Emperor and the Assassin*

## Film Data

Year: 2000
Director: Chen Kaige
Screenplay: Chen Kaige and Wang Peigong
Music: Zhao Jiping
Length: 161 minutes
Rating: R

## Connection to *Patterns of World History* & *Patterns of World History, Brief Edition*

Chapter 9: *China: Imperial Unification and Perfecting the Moral Order*

## Preview

This film dramatizes one of the turning points of Chinese history, the creation of a unified Chinese empire under the leadership of the Qin leader Ying Zheng (Cheng in *Patterns*) in 221 BCE. Determined to bring together, primarily by military force, the seven kingdoms that had been at war with each other for centuries, Zheng ruled Qin from 246 BCE and then the united Chinese empire from 221 to 209 BCE. The particular story of *The Emperor and the Assassin*, derived from the records of the court historian Sima Qian (146–86 BCE), concerned Zheng's mistress, the Lady Zhao, and a fake assassination attempt that was designed to precipitate war between Qin and the Yan kingdom. The film culminates in the destruction of Lady Zhao's homeland, the defeat of Yan, and the crowning of Zheng as Emperor. However, the film also focuses on the Yan assassin, Jing Ke, suggesting the reasons behind the failure of his attempt on Zheng.

The figure of Zheng has been an especially contested one in modern China. Like the Macedonian Philip II, Zheng emerged from the frontiers of Chinese civilization and seized by force its more established cultural centers. His ruthless behavior in annihilating opposition is explained in the film as a result of his difficult childhood as a hostage in Zhao and his single-minded obsession with unifying the country. He is not restrained by love for his mother, his lover, or the children he conquers in his determination to take as much territory as possible. While his empire fell to the Han dynasty 7 years after his death, Zheng had put a halt to the internecine warfare of the states and set the path for a Chinese zenith under the Han. Zheng came into even greater prominence after 1974, when his tomb, containing thousands of terracotta warriors, was discovered under the modern city of Xi'an.

While much of the film's story seems improbable, it is beautifully filmed and was acclaimed outside China as a sweeping historical epic. Like *Confucius* (2010), *The Emperor and the Assassin* is accompanied by a sonorous soundtrack, also scored by Zhao Jiping. Furthermore, the film highlights the importance of Sima Qian as a historian and points up the nature of Chinese historiography, at a time when European historians were creating a similar study in Greco-Roman society.

## Recommended Scenes

➤ Ying Zheng shows his mistress, the Lady Zhao, an enormous map of the empire he is attempting to unite and expresses his dream of a peaceful, law-abiding society, 00:22:43 through 00:30:25.

➤ Lady Zhao travels to the rival kingdom of Yan to find a simulated assassin and discovers a professional killer—now in retirement—called Jing Ke. She works hard to persuade him to come out of retirement, but he is haunted by the memory of an entire family he had killed years earlier, 00:57:45 through 01:03:52.

➤ While in Yan, Lady Zhao receives word that Zheng has invaded her homeland of Zhao. She rushes there to see whether she can save any of the capital's inhabitants and especially its children, 01:48:10 through 01:52:12.

➤ Meeting her lover again, Lady Zhao thinks she has persuaded him to spare the lives of his enemies, but she discovers that he has indeed committed a brutal act of retribution against the city's civilian population, 01:55:36 through 01:58:05.

➤ Now determined to facilitate a real assassination of Zheng, and not merely to provoke a war with Yan, Lady Zhao paves the way for Jing Ke's access to the imperial court. The assassin makes attempts to stab Zheng but is himself murdered, between 02:30:03 and 02:38:35.

## Discussion Questions

1.     Does the film create a completely negative impression of Zheng?

2.     Why does the film provide a backstory and sympathy for the assassin?

3.     Was the personal price Zheng paid worth the unity of his empire?

## Further Reading and Viewing

The contributions of Sima Qian to world history-writing are explored in Georg G. Iggers and Q. Edward Wang's *A Global History of Modern Historiography* (Pearson Longman, 2008), pp. 47–50. A comparison between the ethnographic writing of Sima Qian and the Greek Herodotus (who coined the word 'history') is offered by Siep Stuurman, 'Herodotus and Sima Qian: History and the Anthropological Turn in Ancient Greece and Han China', *Journal of World History* 19 (2008): 1–40.

# *Kingdom of Heaven*

## Film Data

Year: 2005
Director: Ridley Scott
Screenplay: William Monahan
Length: 144 minutes
Rating: R

## Connection to *Patterns of World History* & *Patterns of World History, Brief Edition*

Chapter 10: *Islamic Civilization and Byzantium*

## Preview

*Kingdom of Heaven* is very much a product of its time—and of its (unfortunately) anachronistic hope that a 'heavenly kingdom', characterized by peace between Christians and Muslims, could be installed in the early twenty-first century even though this had failed to materialize in the twelfth. In its broad outlines, the story of the film is based on actual battles and historically attested figures. The central character, Count Balian, was on hand for the Crusaders' defense of Jerusalem against the overwhelming forces of Saladin (Salah ad-Din) in 1187. The screenplay created an improbable backstory for Balian, involving illegitimate birth and a wife's suicide, but the besieged Western Crusaders, or Latin Christians, who attempted to preserve their foothold in Jerusalem are mostly true to history.

Fulfilling the ambitions of Pope Urban II, who had preached a crusade (the term itself was not used in the period, but historians typically refer to this military venture as the First Crusade) to recover the holy sites of Jerusalem from the 'infidels' in 1095, Western Christians sacked Jerusalem in 1099. According to some Crusaders' accounts, their horses waded in the blood of Muslims (and Jews and Eastern Orthodox Christians) up to their bellies in the aftermath of this hyper-violent encounter. While the detail is probably an exaggeration, the loss of life was horrendous—and demanded a counter-response from the

Muslim world, which was, at the time, too fractured and disorganized to mount an effective reconquest of a city that was also sacred to Islam.

By the 1180s, the Crusaders' holdings in the Holy Land had been reduced and—as the film suggests—the Christians of Jerusalem had accommodated themselves and to some extent had assimilated to the prevailing lifestyles and mindsets of their surroundings. Their position was rendered increasingly untenable by the failure of the Second Crusade in the mid-twelfth century and by the poor health of King Baldwin IV, who was a leper without a son and heir. When Baldwin died, power passed to his sister Sibylla and to her husband, Guy de Lusignan. Determined to provoke a war with the gathering forces of Saladin, an ethnic Kurd who had managed to consolidate a substantial segment of the Middle East under his control, Guy and his associate Reynald de Châtillon raided Muslim caravans and committed atrocities against Muslim civilians. When Saladin's sister was captured (at least according to some sources) by one of these raiding parties, tense relations flared into open conflict, and the Crusader army experienced a catastrophic defeat by Saladin's army at Hattin, near the Sea of Galilee. Balian escaped Hattin and energetically defended Jerusalem and its inhabitants for 2 weeks before negotiating terms of surrender to Saladin.

The terms of the negotiation are fascinating and only quickly explored in *Kingdom of Heaven*. Balian threatened to destroy the Muslim holy places in the city, and particularly the famed Dome of the Rock, if Saladin did not accept the surrender of Jerusalem's people and pledge that they would not be killed. Saladin agreed to the terms, but he accepted ransom payments for 'significant' Christians within the city. On the other hand, Balian and Saladin agreed to the enslavement of most of Jerusalem's poorer inhabitants by Muslim traders.

Saladin's reputation as a chivalrous, generous warrior—who could, with justification, have initiated a bloodbath in revenge for the conquest of Jerusalem nearly 90 years earlier—rocketed to prominence in the Christian West. While the surrender of Jerusalem triggered a Third Crusade—which ultimately failed in its aim but occasioned even more horrific massacres and violent deaths in the Holy Land—Saladin became the subject of legends and tales, as a representative of the perfect knight incongruously transplanted to a Christian context.

Fresh from his success with the Roman historical epic *Gladiator* (2000), Ridley Scott turned his attention to this story of Christian–Muslim conflict, which seemed in need of reexamination, particularly in the post-9/11 world. On Sept. 16, 2001, President George W. Bush incited much resentment, though probably inadvertently, by referring to Western efforts against the Taliban in Afghanistan as a 'crusade'. Scott seemed intrigued by the possibility of recreating the Middle East of the late twelfth century, in an attempt to argue for the notion of Christian–Muslim cooperation in a period of—paradoxically?—unremitting violence.

Recollecting his fascination with ancient Rome in the press-book, *Gladiator: The Making of the Ridley Scott Epic* (Newmarket Press, 2000, p. 26), Scott had observed, 'Because what I love to do—apart from getting a good script and making movies—where I enjoy myself most, I think, is creating worlds. Sometimes new worlds, i.e. science fiction, or recreating a world that's historical'. While scholars have generally doubted that he achieved the aim of 'historical accuracy' in *Kingdom of Heaven*, the themes raised in the film are obviously pertinent ones in the first decades of the present millennium.

## Recommended Scenes

➢ The dying father of young Balian (played by Orlando Bloom, even though the historical Balian was in his forties in this period) imparts his vision of a peaceful future between Muslims and Christians, 00:20:41 through 00:24:20. Balian notices that Muslim prayers 'sound like our prayers', and his more ecumenical sensibility is contrasted with the fanatical Guy de Lusignan, who deplores Christian friendships with Muslims.

➢ A Crusader assault on a Muslim caravan occasions an argument over 'what God wills', 00:58:20 through 01:01:45.

➢ Guy de Lusignan longs for a war with Saladin, and Reynald de Châtillon provides the excuse by capturing Saladin's sister. Guy kills Saladin's emissary and war breaks out, between 01:27:00 and 01:29:58.

➢ The defeat of the Crusaders at Hattin is impressively depicted—with circling vultures over the dusty landscape—and Balian prepares to defend Jerusalem. In a crucial, if implausible, speech, Balian insists that Jerusalem's inhabitants matter more than its holy places, 01:36:44 through 01:58:52.

➢ Having defended his city as well as he could (in a thrilling series of scenes depicting medieval siege warfare), Balian surrenders for terms and encounters Saladin in the flesh. In a brief but memorable performance by Ghassan Massoud, Saladin declares that, because he is Saladin, Balian can trust him. Each man recognizes the inherent nobility in the other, and each seems doubtful as to the intrinsic worth of the holy places in the city that is ostensibly sacred to both faiths, 02:04:22 through 02:07:38.

## Discussion Questions

1.    Is the notion of a 'kingdom of heaven' at all realistic, given the endemic religious violence of the twelfth century?

2.    Is the portrait of Saladin in *Kingdom of Heaven* consistent with his image, at least in the Christian West in the Middle Ages?

3.    Is Scott pointing the way to a resolution of conflict in the modern Middle East by means of this film?

## Further Reading and Viewing

Saladin's conquest of Jerusalem is probably best examined from the perspective of Arab chroniclers. A collection of reactions to this event, compiled from Arabic sources, may be found in Francesco Gabrieli's *Arab Historians of the Crusades*, translated by E. J. Costello (Routledge & Kegan Paul, 1969), Part Two: Saladin and the Third Crusade. A biography of *Saladin* by Anne-Marie Eddé, translated by Jane Marie Todd, has recently been published by Harvard University Press (2011).

On *Kingdom of Heaven* in particular, one might consult an essay by Simona Slanička, '*Kingdom of Heaven*—Der Kreuzzug Ridley Scotts gegen den Irakkrieg' ('*Kingdom of Heaven*— Ridley Scott's Crusade against the War in Iraq'), in M. Meier and S. Slanička (eds.), *Antike und Mittelalter im Film: Konstruktion—Dokumentation—Projektion* (Köln: Böhlau Verlag, 2007), pp. 385–397.

# *The Name of the Rose*

## Film Data

Year: 1986
Director: Jean-Jacques Annaud
Based on the novel by Umberto Eco
Production Design: Dante Ferretti
Music: James Horner
Length: 131 minutes
Rating: R

## Connection to *Patterns of World History* & *Patterns of World History, Brief Edition*

Chapter 11: *Innovation and Adaptation in the Western Christian World*

## Preview

This film is described in its opening titles as a 'palimpsest' (a manuscript that has been reused) of the delightful 1980 novel of the same name by Umberto Eco. In addition to being a prolific novelist, Eco is also a professor of semiotics at the Università di Bologna, and there is a sly reference in the film to a manuscript containing the annotations of an 'Umberto di Bologna'. Such quick and witty allusions are a hallmark of Eco's style, and *The Name of the Rose* was far more than a conventional murder mystery set in the Middle Ages. Even the title of the book hints at Eco's professional fascination with words and their meaning, since the full sentence referred to is, 'All that remains of a dead rose is the name'. (The quote is drawn from a twelfth-century Benedictine monk's poem *De contemptu mundi*, 'On Contempt for the World'.)

In an interview about the film in the 1980s, Eco observed that his novel—though set in a northern Italian monastery in 1327—addressed a 'time of uncertainty' that was very much like our own time. The world, and particularly the intellectual world, was undergoing a profound transition, and Eco diagnosed this transition as one out of blind faith (literally, in that its main exponent is the blind monk Jorge) and into logic, reason, and the erasure of superstition. Eco named the novel's hero and primary investigator of the mystery William of Baskerville, and the Sherlock Holmesian allusions are carried to their logical extension when William actually comments to his Watson-like assistant monk, 'Elementary, my dear Adso'. As Conan Doyle's great detective had pursued logic and reason wherever they led in his investigations, Eco suggested that a similarly incisive mind could have solved murders nearly 600 years earlier. Such a man would, in all probability, have been associated with the institutional Church, and yet, because he attributed the deaths to human agency rather than to supernatural forces, he might have been considered a heretic by his more fanatical contemporaries.

A multinational European production, headed by the French director Annaud, attempted to bring the novel to the screen, and Eco praised Annaud's team for 'creating a world around the mystery' he had sketched out. Consulting with the famous medievalist Jacques Le Goff, Annaud strove for historical authenticity in 'tous les éléments matériels' ('all the material elements'), as Le Goff commented. In the film, the Middle Ages itself became a character, and elaborate sets were constructed outside Rome, at Cinecittà, and at Eberbach near the German Rhine. An international cast, headed by Sean Connery as William, was assembled, and filming went on briskly and efficiently as the body count mounted up on screen. A satisfying conclusion of the mystery wraps up the details of the murders, but William's identification of the killer leads to a fire in the monastery that destroys untold numbers of priceless manuscripts in its secret library. Such accidents must have resulted in real losses for all of us, and Annaud may have been implying that cultural progress is fragile and remains similarly at risk in today's world.


## Recommended Scenes

➤ The Franciscan friar William of Baskerville and his assistant Adso have come to an Italian monastery to attend a debate, set against the backdrop of tension between the Emperor and the Pope (this monastery owes allegiance to the Pope in Avignon, a reference to the 'Babylonian captivity' of the Church).

➤ When he arrives, the abbot informs William of a problem that has befallen his monastery in recent days, the unsolved mystery surrounding the death of a young manuscript illuminator. The scene also introduces the element of diabolical influence and the forces of religious fundamentalism, between 00:08:22 through 00:15:33.

➢ While William pursues his investigations into the death, measuring footprints and looking for clues, two more deaths occur, and these seem much more likely to be murders. The discovery of the victims' blackened fingers and tongues suggests a connection between the monks' habit of licking their fingers while reading and their deaths. Accordingly, reading—at least when the books are poisoned—can literally be deadly, as developed between 01:00:10 and 01:06:15.

➢ William and Adso discover the fantastic and stuffed secret library in the monastery, and William exults in the number of books, generally considered lost, that are available in the library stacks, 01:13:08 through 01:20:45.

➢ Papal envoys arrive, and a debate commences about whether Jesus owned his own cloak. The debate is—and is designed to be—esoteric in the extreme, but there is a serious issue at its heart. This is essentially whether the Church itself should have possessions or renounce them and adopt a lifestyle of poverty, as the Franciscans officially had. In the midst of this debate another monk is murdered, 01:30:55 through 01:34:54.

➢ The murderer is unveiled, and he insists that the murders were justified to prevent the dissemination of unholy knowledge. A fire in the library results in the destruction of even more learning, but William manages to save a few volumes before exiting the building, 01:47:33 through 02:04:46.

## Discussion Questions

1.    How does the theme of ecclesiastical poverty relate to the lives of the impoverished peasants who live around the monastery?

2.    To what extent was knowledge considered dangerous in the Middle Ages? What sort of knowledge?

3.    What role does laughter have in the use of reason? Why is Jorge so opposed to it, whether literally indulged in the scriptorium or justified in the library's books?

## Further Reading and Viewing

The 2004 DVD release of the film includes a West German documentary on its production, entitled 'Die Abtei des Verbrechens' ('The Abbey of Crime'). Produced in 1986, this short film contains the expected behind-the-scenes footage, but it focuses primarily on the novelist Eco, the director Jean-Jacques Annaud, and the script advisor, historian Jacques Le Goff. Those curious about Eco's style and method should also consult the original novel, together with his many other novels, including *Foucault's Pendulum* (1988) and his most recent, *The Prague Cemetery* (2010). The latter is a novelistic treatment of the actual characters involved in the creation of the deadly 'Protocols of the Elders of Zion'.

# *Mongol*

## Film Data

Year: 2007
Director: Sergei Bodrov
Screenplay: Sergei Bodrov and Arif Aliyev
Length: 125 minutes
Rating: R

## Connection to *Patterns of World History* & *Patterns of World History, Brief Edition*

Chapter 12: *Contrasting Patterns in India and China*

## Preview

*Mongol* is a biographical treatment of Genghis Khan (here referred to by his Mongol name, Temujin), from his childhood until his conquest of other Mongolian tribes in the 1190s. The film does not carry the story forward to his conquest of much of Asia, from China to the Caspian Sea, but it does give a sense of the brutality of the culture that shaped him and how determined he was to overcome the suffering inflicted upon him as a child and young adult.

Over the course of the film, the viewer is given a sense of the enormous vistas of the steppe-land of interior Asia, and horses gallop at top speed across a vast and desolate landscape. The yurts, animals, and heavy fur-lined coats of the Mongols are all present in the film, and they give evidence to the harsh terrain and forbidding environment that created a tough and proud warrior culture among the Mongols. Shooting in Mongolia, China, and Kazakhstan, Bodrov provides insight into the Mongolian language and its customs, at least at this stage of history, and he depicts the origins of the Mongol horsemen rather than the results of their raids on other cultures.

A particularly striking element in *Mongol* is its attention to the Mongol code of behavior. Repeatedly, characters comment that 'Mongols do' or 'Mongols do not' behave in certain ways. While the culture may appear brutal and 'uncivilized', the Mongols did have a code of honor that demanded swift and effective punishment if violated.

## Recommended Scenes

➤ When Temujin is 9 years old, his father, the Khan of a Mongol tribe, is poisoned by his enemies. The young boy's village is raided, and he is abducted into a life of slavery and suffering, 00:10:16 through 00:17:58.

➤ After years of escape and recapture, Temujin is reunited with his fiancée. However, she is soon abducted by a rival clan, prompting Temujin to exact a terrible vengeance on their village in her rescue, 00:41:08 through 00:54:37.

➤ After another series of reversals, a Chinese lord from the kingdom of Tangut buys Temujin as a slave and keeps him in a cage to be mocked by the residents of Tangut. A Buddhist monk agrees to help Temujin, in exchange for his protection should he ever conquer Tangut, 01:20:05 through 01:25:17.

➤ Broken out of his cage and reunited with his wife and children, Temujin gives voice to his plan to unite the Mongols and provide them with a legal system—even if 'I must kill half of them to do it', 01:41:50 through 01:47:07.

➤ Having defeated his enemies in a major battle, Temujin articulates his future plans, and captions refer to his ultimate conquest (and annihilation) of Tangut, along with many other countries, 01:59:10 through 02:01:27.

## Discussion Questions

1.    Does the film suggest that the Mongols were not completely 'uncivilized'?

2.    How did the Mongol code of honor work?

3.    How does Temujin propose to achieve Mongol unity?

## Further Reading and Viewing

A revisionist and generally sympathetic biography can be found in Jack Weatherford's *Genghis Khan and the Making of the Modern World* (Crown Publishers, 2004). In 2003, DNA evidence revealed that roughly 16 million males alive today (or 0.5% of the globe's male population) are biological descendants of Genghis Khan.

# *Kagemusha (The Shadow Warrior)*

## Film Data

Year: 1980
Director: Akira Kurosawa
Screenplay: Akira Kurosawa and Masato Ide
Length: 180 minutes
Rating: PG

## Connection to *Patterns of World History* & *Patterns of World History, Brief Edition*

Chapter 13: *Religious Civilizations Interacting: Korea, Japan, and Vietnam*

Chapter 21: *Regulating the "Inner" and "Outer" Domains: China and Japan*

## Preview

*Kagemusha* helped to solidify the reputation of Akira Kurosawa as one of the global masters of cinematic art, but it also illustrates a significant period of Japanese history. Set in the years just before and during the Battle of Nagashino (June 1575), the film underscores the instability of the '*Gekokujo*' ('those below toppling those above') age that preceded the installation of the Tokugawa regime in 1600. The fictional story, based initially on over 200 images that Kurosawa had painted, concerns a double or '*kagemusha*', who impersonates the Takeda Shingen in the years before Nagashino. Shingen was known to have employed doubles, and the notion of a double who impersonates a leader so well that he takes the place of the original is a familiar one from many tales. One of the best of these is Lion Feuchtwanger's 1936 novel, *Der falsche Nero* [*The False Nero*], in which a luckless man impersonates the Roman emperor Nero and then reprises his role after Nero is thought to be dead.

However, Kurosawa's original idea—which would allow him to cast an actor in a double role and to experiment with bold color patterns drawn from his paintings—hit a roadblock in the 1970s. Despite his prominence for a string of critically acclaimed 'samurai' films in the 1950s and 1960s, Kurosawa's recent films had been disappointing, and he had withdrawn into a semiretirement. Nevertheless, his admirers in the United States were determined that Kurosawa would secure funding for this new project. Because these admirers included Francis Ford Coppola, director of *The Godfather* (1972), and George Lucas, who had made a stratospheric hit with *Star Wars* (1977), obtaining the financing proved to be no difficulty.

Incorporating the vibrant color of his own paintings into the final product, Kurosawa experimented with unusual filters, camera angles, and lush dream sequences, attempting, as he observed, to reproduce 'the images I saw in my mind'. Nevertheless, the film is also full of period detail, including the European Catholic missionaries who began to appear in southern Japan in the 1540s and are represented in *Kagemusha* by priests and even a cardinal's hat carried on a spear. The scenario also draws attention to the disorder of the period and the limits of '*bushido*', the warrior code of honor that supposedly dictated proper behavior for the samurai. As in *Rashomon* (1950), this film demonstrates that ideal codes might break down in real situations.

## Recommended Scenes

➢ Due to a fortuitous similarity of appearance with the leader of the Takeda clan, a thief is spared from execution, and the idea of his acting as a double is aired, between 00:00:42 and 00:07:14.

➢ Shingen encourages his soldiers, and Kurosawa employs the images of brilliant sunlight against a red sky, 00:21:15 through 00:25:08.

➢ Once Shingen has died, his brother Nobukado remembers the double and proposes that he pose as Shingen, at least for a few years. While the double manages to fool the soldiers and spies from other clans who have come to observe, it is clear that he will be difficult to handle, 00:35:21 through 00:43:54.

➢ Once he discovers (while attempting to steal a jar containing Shingen's body) that the clan leader is actually dead, the double begins to have a change of heart, understanding that the imposture is not a mere joke, but could actually benefit his region.

➢ At a conference of the Takeda clan, the impostor is nearly exposed, but quick thinking saves the day, 01:42:49 through 01:53:57.

➢ In an impressive battle scene, shot from above and at ground level, the double acts as Shingen, but he comes to see the cost of war in the dead soldiers around him. The deception is exposed when he falls from his horse, and his mistress does not find the scar she knows should be there, 02:12:00 through 02:20:33.

➢ The signature moments of the film are in its final sequences, between 02:39:20 and 02:57:40, detailing the Battle of Nagashino which resulted in catastrophe for the Takeda. In an innovative technique, the actual battlefield deaths are not shown, but the camera focuses on the reactions of those watching wave after wave of men being killed. The final, stunning visuals are of men and horses trying to struggle up from the ground as they lie dying, and then the thief himself is killed. His body floats down the river over a banner holding the words of Sun Tzu.

## Discussion Questions

1.      Why does the thief experience a change of heart in the course of his impersonation?

2.      What does the film suggest about the nature of war?

3.      Does the film challenge the relevance of the supposed *bushido* code?

## Further Reading and Viewing

The Criterion DVD of the film, released in 2005, contains an extra disc of special features, placing the film within the context of Kurosawa's body of work and against the specific circumstances of the late 1970s. George Lucas and Francis Ford Coppola introduce the film and comment on their support in producing it.

# *Yeelen (Brightness)*

## Film Data

Year: 1987
Director: Souleymane Cissé
Length: 105 minutes
Rating: No rating

## Connection to *Patterns of World History* & *Patterns of World History, Brief Edition*

Chapter 14: *Patterns of State Formation in Africa*

## Preview

*Yeelen* is already a classic statement in modern African cinema and a tribute to the creativity of both its director, Souleymane Cissé, and the Malian film industry, which has produced critically acclaimed projects like *Guimba the Tyrant* (1995) and *Bamako* (2006) in recent years. The film is specifically concerned with the religious beliefs and practices of the Bambara people in the (European) medieval period, and it treats the spells and magical powers of individuals seriously and without condescension. The central sacred objects in the film are a long pole and a decorated plank, which emits the 'brightness' that provides the culminating scene. Throughout, *Yeelen* shows the practice of Bambara religion, and the belief structure that lay behind it, to tell a story that touches on magic, sorcery, and father–son conflict.

*Yeelen* is based on a thirteenth-century Malian legend concerning a father who possesses magical powers and is jealous of his son, who possesses the same, and perhaps superior, powers. Niankoro's father Soma has pledged to kill his son and, in the opening scene, he appeals to the god Mari, resident in the wooden object, to help him track down and kill Niankoro. The young man's mother counteracts this with her own religious offerings to the 'Goddess of the Waters', and Niankoro has a series of adventures and reversals before finally encountering his father.

The film attempts to recreate both the spiritual and the physical life of the Bambara people in this period, providing insight into gender relations (especially through Niankoro's relationship with his wife Attu) and governmental structures. It was deliberately filmed in the Bambara language and not in French, the colonial language of Mali, and it featured nonprofessional actors in many roles. The impending history of the Malian people, in terms of the slave trade and the erasure of their cultural identity, is foreshadowed by Niankoro's blind uncle Djigui, and the film attests to the vibrancy and brilliance of this civilization before its encounter with Europeans.

## Recommended Scenes

➤ Soma uses his wooden god to break down the door of the hut from which Niankoro and his mother have just escaped, 00:02:04 through 00:11:21.

➤ Guided by a mysterious man in a tree with a gorilla's head, Niankoro is captured by herders but demonstrates his supernatural powers to their king, 00:20:53 through 00:30:47.

➤ Enjoined to counteract the presumed barrenness of the king's youngest wife Attu, Niankoro sleeps with the woman, and she becomes pregnant. The king gives Attu to Niankoro, and they go into exile together, between 00:47:53 and 00:57:21.

➤ The young man's uncle predicts that Attu will have a son, but that disaster will soon come and enslavement will befall their people, 01:18:31 through 01:26:34.

➤ When the father and son finally confront each other, their magical wooden objects are brought to the contest as well. An overwhelming brightness emanates from the plank, blinding and incinerating both father and son. Two white globes (perhaps the eggs of future magicians?) are left behind; Attu picks up one of these and walks away, 01:34:53 through 01:41:50.

## Discussion Questions

1.    Does the film seem to suggest that the magic of the Bambara is 'real'?

2.    How are the religious practices of the Bambara people demonstrated?

3.    What does the film suggest about gender relations among the Bambara?

## Further Reading and Viewing

A 2010 essay on *Yeelen* by David-Pierre Fila, entitled '*Yeelen* ou la sorcellerie filmée' ('*Yeelen* or Filmed Sorcery'), can be found online at http://www.africine.org/?menu=art&no=9545.

# *Kings of the Sun*

## Film Data

Year: 1963
Director: J. Lee Thompson
Length: 108 minutes
Rating: No rating

## Connection to *Patterns of World History* & *Patterns of World History, Brief Edition*

Chapter 15: *The Rise of Empires in the Americas*

## Preview

This film explores—though not in a terribly sophisticated or convincing manner—the possibility of Mayan migration from the vicinity of Chichén Itzá to the coastal areas of the northern Gulf of Mexico in the early thirteenth century. It opens with the invasion of the rival Mayan leader Hunac Ceel, which probably did take place in this period, and it introduces the central character Balam, a name that is likely derived from the Mayan Book of Chilam Balam of Chunayel. After Hunac Ceel's invasion, Balam leads his people through a secret passage under Chichén Itzá to the coast, persuading them to take to boats and sail north until they reach another shore. The remainder of the film chronicles Balam's attempt to rebuild his culture on the Gulf Coast of today's southern United States, while also confronting the local inhabitants, who eventually come to welcome the Mayan settlers.

Accordingly, the bulk of the film is fanciful and characterized by the unintentionally ludicrous notion that the Mayans and Yul Brynner's 'Black Eagle' would speak the same dialect of English (though, in Black Eagle's case, refracted through the broken English that generally accompanied Native Americans in film Westerns). Nevertheless, archaeology has confirmed at least some points of contact between the inhabitants of the Yucatán and various Mississippian cultures in the interior of North America. *Patterns of History* notes that an obsidian scraper transported from the Valley of Mexico to the Spiro Mounds in modern

Oklahoma suggests at least occasional contact between Mesoamerican and Mississippian cultures in this period. Unfortunately, the film also perpetuates stereotypes about the supposedly bloodthirsty Mesoamerican cultures, who were invariably addicted to human sacrifice. On the other hand, it intimates that the Mayans eventually became more 'civilized' and decided to abandon the practice.

*Kings of the Sun* is not a historical film per se, but it does reflect some of the attitudes and prejudices of its era, particularly in respect to Native Americans. Black Eagle's tribe speaks in the language audiences had come to expect from Native Americans in film, and their tipis, battle cries, and clothing reinforce rather than undermine these racist stereotypes. However, the film does point out the need for people of various religious and ethnic backgrounds to find common goals and work together to adapt to a new environment. Thus the hints of a more tolerant, globalized era may be contained in this film, even if they are subsumed in the blazing sun of the Gulf.

## Recommended Scenes

➤ Balam leads his followers away from Chichén Itzá, following a legend of land in the far north across the sea, 00:07:02 through 00:17:35.

➤ Black Eagle spies the new settlers on his land and reports to his own people that this is the leading edge of a larger invasion force, 00:26:18 through 00:29:31.

➤ The Mayans capture Black Eagle on his scouting expedition and plan to sacrifice him in their new temple, 00:34:55 through 00:43:13.

➤ Balam decides to free Black Eagle, who returns to his people and proposes a treaty of friendship with the Mayans, between 01:05:20 through 01:18:15.

➤ Hunac Ceel crosses the sea with his own invasion force and attacks the Mayan settlement. Black Eagle helps his new friends against the invader and dies in their defense, 01:39:30 through 01:47:25.

## Discussion Questions

1.      How does the film address the issue of human sacrifice, and why?

2.      What other stories of migration is *Kings of the Sun* intended to recall?

3.      What significance would Black Eagle and his people have had, specifically for audiences in the United States?

## Further Reading and Viewing

An English translation of the Book of Chilam Balam, published in 1933, is available online at:

http://theknowledgeden.com/wp-content/uploads/2011/11/Book-of-Chilam-Balam-the-of-Chumayel.-By-Ralph-L-Roys-1933.-Etext.pdf.

# La Otra Conquista (The Other Conquest)

## Film Data

Year: 2000
Director and Screenwriter: Salvador Carrasco
Length: 105 minutes
Rating: R

## Connection to *Patterns of World History* & *Patterns of World History, Brief Edition*

Chapter 15: *The Rise of Empires in the Americas*

Chapter 18: *New Patterns in New Worlds: Colonialism and Indigenous Responses in the Americas*

## Preview

This brilliant study of Aztec cultural resistance to the Spanish conquest of the early sixteenth century takes on the form of 'another' or a 'counter' conquest. The specific contention of *La Otra Conquista* is that indigenous and European cultural values were fused together in new and creative ways in the aftermath of the violent suppression of the Aztec empire. It also suggests, through the character of the Aztec artist and scribe Topiltzin, the possible origins of the Mexican icon the Virgin of Guadalupe, as a combination of the Virgin Mary and the Aztec mother goddess. Moreover, it strongly hints that Friar Diego, who is initially determined to convert the pagan Aztecs, has lost his faith in the universal Christian God as a result of his encounter with Topiltzin. While it is primarily fictional, the film introduces historical figures like Hernán Cortés and Tecuichpotzin, the daughter of the Aztec king Moctezuma II who lived with Cortés as Doña Isabel.

Mexican director Carrasco strove for authenticity in the production, and the actors portraying Aztec characters were instructed in the pronunciation of the native language Nahuatl. In an interview about the film, Carrasco claimed that Mexican authorities were initially opposed to his filming at pre-Columbian and colonial sites in the country but that they eventually relented. While the script is intelligent, lively, and full of insight into the history of the period, the visual imagery is equally compelling. Topiltzin's inner life is often explained visually, with no spoken dialogue, and the score melds European and Aztec music together to heighten the theme of cultural fusion. The artistic life of Topiltzin is also handled in a clever way, as it posits the origins for some of the images in the famous codices emanating from Aztec civilization.

The film is also remarkable for addressing, in a more sophisticated way than Mel Gibson's *Apocalypto* (2006), the notion of human sacrifice in pre-Columbian societies. In a scene of human sacrifice that is interrupted by the Spaniards, an Aztec woman willingly and knowingly gives herself to the sacrifice. Here and elsewhere, the film intercuts images of this victim with the Virgin Mary, underscoring the theme of self-sacrifice in both the Aztec and Christian religions. As Carrasco observed, the native population of Mexico was probably reduced to 10% of its pre-Columbian levels, but remnants of its beliefs were absorbed into the religious and cultural life of the 'New World'.

## Recommended Scenes

➢ Captions set the scene for the early phases of the film, in the 2 years after the conquest of Tenochtitlán by the Spanish in 1519. An image from an Aztec codex floats out of a dying friar's Bible, and a flashback explains its origin in a massacre of Aztecs by the Spaniards, 00:02:01 through 00:09:32.

➢ A human sacrifice is interrupted, and Topiltzin's remaining family members are murdered or captured. His codex is burned, and Friar Diego, newly arrived from Spain, is told, 'You'll never convert these people', between 00:19:32 and 00:28:13.

➢ Topiltzin's life is saved by the intervention of Tecuichpotzin, who claims, probably falsely, that he is her half-brother. He is, however, beaten, tortured, and forcibly converted to Christianity, as a tear steals down the face of a statue of the Virgin Mary, 00:44:58 through 00:55:14.

➢ Topiltzin, now forced to live in a monastery as Brother Tomás, is searching for meaning and begins to fuse the image of the Virgin with those of the Aztec goddess and the other Aztec women in his life, 01:10:50 through 01:19:44.

➢ Topiltzin challenges the Christian God, as he had his own Sun-God at the film's beginning. Friar Diego goes on his own quest to discover Topiltzin's religion, with the strains of a Nahualtl aria sounding around him, 01:22:58 through 01:28:10.

➢ Topiltzin removes his Christian habit, reassumes a native loincloth, and steals the statue of the Virgin from the sacristy. Removing her crown, he falls—perhaps deliberately—with the statue and is killed. Friar Diego sees the white face of the statue lying beside the native face of the dead Topiltzin, between 01:36:32 and 01:46:42.

## Discussion Questions

1.    How does the film describe the fusion of the Catholic and Aztec religions?

2.    What does the film suggest was the role of art in the preservation of Aztec culture?

3.    Does Friar Diego lose his Christian faith by the end of the film?

## Further Reading and Viewing

The 2007 DVD release contains a superb audio commentary track (in English) by the director. The success of Carrasco's film has paved the way for the mainstream acceptance of Mexican filmmakers like Alfonso Cuarón, Guillermo del Toro, and Alejandro González Iñárritu.

# *Dangerous Beauty*

## Film Data

Year: 1998
Director: Marshall Herskovitz
Based on the book *The Honest Courtesan* (1992), by Margaret F. Rosenthal
Length: 111 minutes
Rating: R

## Connection to *Patterns of World History* & *Patterns of World History, Brief Edition*

Chapter 16: *The Ottoman–Habsburg Struggle and Western European Overseas Expansion*

## Preview

*Dangerous Beauty* is a highly dramatized (and comically salacious) rendering of Rosenthal's scholarly study of the life and works of the Venetian courtesan/poet Veronica Franco (1546–1591). The bulk of Rosenthal's biography focuses on Franco's poetry, which was unusual for having been published and having brought her a degree of fame and notoriety, and on her two appearances before the Inquisition in 1580. The majority of the film, as one might expect, deals with Franco's energetic sexual encounters, and it stresses her relative freedom, as a prostitute allowed to frequent the company of high-born Venetian men in contrast to the married women of the city. Nevertheless, the film does touch on three themes developed in this chapter on Ottoman–Habsburg struggle, especially in the Mediterranean context.

First, the presence of Ottomans, whether real or imagined, is palpable in the background of *Dangerous Beauty*, and the war between Venice and the Ottoman Empire over Cyprus (1570–1573) furnishes important plot points. Turkish men with their characteristic headdress appear at a Venetian masked ball early in the film, and several of Veronica's lovers mention the intentions of the Sultan and Venice's plans to thwart them. Her long-term lover

Marco Venier is sent to the war, only to return—at least in the film—in the midst of a plague that has hit Venice in 1575–1577.

The film also makes a solid case for the role of Veronica as a diplomat on Venice's behalf, particularly in her dealing with the French king Henri III. Henri did visit Venice for 10 days in July 1574, and it is clear that Franco spent time with him, whether on intimate terms or not. The film suggests—rather crudely—that the encounter was primarily if unusually sexual in nature, but it does not mention Franco's two sonnets and a dedicatory letter addressed to the king at some point after his visit. *Dangerous Beauty* underscores the relationship between the courtesan and the monarch, intimating that Franco acted on behalf of her city and scored a diplomatic victory with her unique talents. However, it should be noted that Venice had already joined Christian monarchs, from the Habsburg emperors to the Valois kings, in a 'Holy Christian League' that had secured a major victory at Lepanto in 1571.

Most significantly, the film draws significant attention to the role of women in Mediterranean societies, from regions dominated by both Christianity and Islam. As her mother, herself a former courtesan, reminds Veronica, powerful women like Aspasia and Cleopatra had used their sexual prowess to achieve status for themselves in a world similarly dominated by men. By surrendering her dream of a stable, conventional married life, which was not suitable to a woman in her social position, Veronica could be party to the conversations, intellectual pursuits, and international diplomacy of men. While the life of an average prostitute, even in luxurious Venice, must have been far less glamorous, Veronica escapes the traditional boundaries placed on women in her age and achieves a full artistic life—over the objections of moral puritans and even of Church authorities.

## Recommended Scenes

➢ Veronica's mother introduces her to the greatest benefit of being a courtesan, the securing of an education, between 00:17:40 and 00:24:35.

➢ Veronica, in bed with a cardinal, hears of the beginning of war with the Ottomans, bids farewell to her lover Marco, and exercises her diplomacy with Henri III, 01:01:43 through 01:17:10.

➢ After her mother has died of plague, Veronica is harassed by newly puritanical Venetians and hauled before the Inquisition. She does, however, manage to scratch out her poetry on the prison walls, 01:27:20 through 01:31:22.

> In a highly fictitious but nicely imagined scene the men of Venice defend Veronica against the Church Inquisitors, 01:40:45 through 01:48:08.

## Discussion Questions

1.    Are the Turks in this film merely a sinister presence threatening the health and security of Venice?

2.    Is *Dangerous Beauty* too celebratory of the lives of prostitutes in early modern Europe?

3.    Does the film underscore the dangers of religious fundamentalism and sexual puritanism?

## Further Reading and Viewing

Margaret Rosenthal's *The Honest Courtesan* (University of Chicago Press, 1992) provides all of the essential details for Veronica Franco's unique life, work, and times. The cover image of the book is Tintoretto's portrait of her, and the book contains many printed samples and translations of her poetry together with extensive illustrations.

# La Reine Margot (Queen Margot)

## Film Data

Year: 1994
Director: Patrice Chéreau
Screenplay: Danièle Thompson and Patrice Chéreau
Music: Goran Bregovic
Length: 144 minutes
Rating: R

## Connection to *Patterns of World History* & *Patterns of World History, Brief Edition*

Chapter 17: *Renaissance, Reformation, and the New Science in Europe*

## Preview

The St. Bartholomew's Day Massacre, launched on August 23, 1572, was a watershed and emblematic event in the French Wars of Religion. This series of violent attacks and reprisals began in 1562 and killed tens of thousands of Catholics and Huguenots (French Calvinists) until Henri IV Bourbon declared that '*Paris vaut bien une messe*' ('Paris is worth a mass') and issued the Edict of Nantes in 1598. The murder of roughly 2,000 Protestants in a Paris that was still celebrating the marriage of the Catholic princess Marguerite de Valois to the Protestant Henri de Navarre triggered even more violence outside the capital for the next several weeks.

The image of thousands of rotting corpses in the August heat was an inescapable one for playwrights, painters, novelists, and, eventually, filmmakers. Christopher Marlowe produced his play *The Massacre at Paris* in 1593, commenting obliquely on how differently matters stood in England in this period, and D. W. Griffith in his influential silent film *Intolerance* (1916) would profile the Massacre as one of four historical incidents of intolerance in action. However, the strongest artistic statement on the Massacre remains the novel *La Reine Margot* (*Queen Margot*), published by Alexandre Dumas *père* in 1845. The novel conflates several historical characters and creates an improbable romance between the Princess

Marguerite (Margot) and a Protestant whose life she saves on that fateful night, but at its core there is a compelling plea for religious tolerance and understanding.

In the 1990s, Patrice Chéreau decided to revisit the story of this classic novel, perhaps because a call for tolerance across religious divides seemed more relevant than ever. The degree to which Muslim citizens of France are threatened by the Republican tradition of '*laïcité*' ('secularism') continues to be a matter of debate. Occasionally centered on religious garb, appearance, or language, the debate is connected to wider issues of assimilation, tolerance, and relationships across community lines. By demonstrating the full force of religious violence, accompanied by brutal sixteenth-century weapons and copious amounts of blood, the filmmakers may have hoped to underscore the possible consequences of intolerance in today's world.

The highlight of the film is certainly the 15-minute sequence detailing the scope of the massacre, accompanied by powerful music and visceral language. Furthermore, the film is brilliantly cast, particularly in its female leads, Isabelle Adjani as Margot and the Italian actress Virna Lisi as the Queen Mother, Catherine de Medici. Lisi's Italian accent—appropriate for a French queen whose family originated in Florence—is strong and strengthens at moments of tension especially when she shouts at her weak son, Charles IX, and her daughter Margot. The French '*besoin*' ('need') slips slightly into the Italian '*bisogna*' when she explains, echoing Niccolò Macchiavelli (another Florentine), the occasional necessity of swift and brutal action to forestall a worse disaster. *La Reine Margot* draws attention to the fact that Catherine's scheming will only result in the extinction of her family and the succession of the hated 'peasant' Henri Bourbon.


## Recommended Scenes

➢ Captions explain the religious conflict, ongoing for many years before 1572, and the forced wedding between Marguerite and Henri is depicted in full, and often amusing, detail, 00:01:55 through 00:10:05.

➢ After an assassination attempt against the Protestant leader Coligny fails, a family conference decides to cover up the evidence by launching a massacre of all Protestants resident in Paris. Against the backdrop of ringing bells, screams, and gunshots, the violent night unfolds, between 00:39:20 and 00:56:46.

➢ Catherine's new son-in-law Henri, even though he is the Huguenot leader of a small independent country, survives the night's horrors, but he is forced to convert—at least nominally—to Catholicism. Margot is still covered with the blood of a man whose life she saved in the palace, 00:57:22 through 01:00:17.

➢ This man, a largely fictional character called La Mole, is left for dead, still clutching a Catholic with whom he had dueled. The public executioner, noticing that the men have been dumped into a common grave but are still alive, rescues them, and the two former enemies become fast and committed friends, 01:17:20 through 01:26:05.

➤ In an innovative twist on the historical record, Charles IX is mistakenly poisoned by a book left for Henri. Charles' mother Catherine is the villainess in the piece, and she has now managed to kill her eldest son, paving the way for the accession of her favorite son as Henri III, 02:00:30 through 02:07:17.

➤ La Mole and his friend Coconnas are executed, but Margot takes La Mole's head with her to exile in Navarre. A Hebrew song closes the film, and captions tell the viewer that her husband Henri will become Henri IV in 1589, 02:14:30 through 02:17:40.

## Discussion Questions

1.    What motivates the orgy of violence on the night of the Massacre?

2.    Why does Henri de Navarre convert and reconvert so often?

3.    What are the contemporary resonances of the bells rung in August 1572?

## Further Reading and Viewing

A superb collection of documents regarding the Massacre and its results is available in Barbara B. Diefendorf's *The Saint Bartholomew's Day Massacre: A Brief History with Documents* (Bedford/St. Martin's, 2009). Some of the same territory is covered in the 2010 film *La princesse de Montpensier* (*The Princess of Montpensier*), which is similarly inspired by a historical novel covering the events of the Massacre and in particular its effect on the Guise family.

# *Black Robe*

## Film Data

Year: 1991
Director: Bruce Beresford
Screenplay: Brian Moore, based on his novel
Length: 101 minutes
Rating: R

## Connection to *Patterns of World History* & *Patterns of World History, Brief Edition*

Chapter 18: *New Patterns in New Worlds: Colonialism and Indigenous Responses in the Americas*

## Preview

*Black Robe* is a cinematic rendering of Brian Moore's 1985 novel, focusing on the experiences of the Jesuit Father Laforgue in New France (Québec and Ontario) in the 1630s. Father Laforgue feels driven to convert and civilize the native peoples of the St. Lawrence basin, and he encounters widely varying responses to his mission among the Algonquin, Huron, and Iroquois peoples. While the novel is a work of fiction, its basic substance is inspired by specific incidents contained in the famous *Jesuit Relations*, which were published in Paris between 1632 and 1673.

When the French established a fort at what would become Québec City in 1608, they came into contact with established indigenous confederations, but some Catholic groups in France detected in this incursion into North America a new mission field, ripe for harvest by energetic, and very brave, young priests. The French had a light and thin administrative presence, and they were forced to interact and trade with the First Nations peoples surrounding them. North America would later become the scene of bitter colonial struggles between the French, Dutch, and English, but the film focuses particularly on the determination of some to share Christianity with people who had very little interest in giving up their 'savage' beliefs.

While there were only two Jesuits in Québec in 1632, thirty to forty would be active in New France by the 1640s. Recruited from Jesuit colleges in France, they were seen as the leading edge of 'civilization' in the region, though they were often, as in other parts of the world, subjected to brutal reprisals by native peoples. The level and brutality of the violence directed against them seemed to reinforce, in some minds, the 'savagery' that dominated these cultures, and this strengthened calls to continue the missions. The end result of this contact was, as in many regions touched by Europeans, death on an unimaginable scale, due to disease as well as to violent subjugation.

The film, like the novel that inspires it, asks clear and pointed questions about who were the civilized in this historical moment and who the savages. The languages, stories, and religions of the various native peoples are showcased, and their religious officials battle for the hearts and minds of their people with Father Laforgue. In the course of the novel, Laforgue is beaten, has a finger severed by a shell with a sharp edge, and suffers cold, hunger, and abandonment. Nevertheless, at the end of the film, he can declare that he does, after all, love the people of New France and is still committed to sharing Christianity with them.

The story of Laforgue is inspired by many separate accounts in the *Jesuit Relations*, coupled with Moore's superb imagination, but the closest historical parallel is probably Jean de Brébeuf. Jean was tortured and killed during an Iroquois invasion of Huron territory (in today's southern Ontario) in 1649 and then made a saint in the Catholic Church. He had spent many years among the Hurons, learning their language and operating missions among them from 1626 to 1629 and again from 1634 until his murder in 1649. The missions founded among the Hurons were sometimes successful and sometimes abandoned, often due to outbreaks of disease. When influenza killed a great many Hurons in 1637, the Jesuits were suspected of spreading the disease deliberately, through some sort of black magic, and several French people were killed.

Images of Brébeuf with burning axe blades seared into his body, placed alongside pictures of other Jesuits being burned alive or hacked to death with their already-mutilated fingers clasped in prayer, reinforced European notions of the 'uncivilized' nature of First Nations peoples. However, this film casts the story differently, asking whether the 'Black Robes', the term applied to the priests by the bewildered natives, should have attempted this conversion at all.

## Recommended Scenes

➢ The credits open over seventeenth-century maps of the St. Lawrence and Great Lakes region, and the drawings of violence by native people and the identification of a settlement of '*sorciers*' ('magicians') is noted on the map, 00:00:42 through 00:04:22. The date of the film, 1634, is given, together with a sense of the region's recent past.

➢ The French under Samuel de Champlain and the Algonquin prepare for a conference, and the film stresses the similarity of their preparations, as both groups employ clothes, gifts, and music before and during their diplomacy, 00:08:21 through 00:14:22. Champlain manages to persuade the Algonquin to send a small escort force of their people to accompany Father Laforgue to the Huron mission.

➢ Father Laforgue attempts to explain the concept of Heaven and elements of the French language to his escort party and to representatives of another people, the Montagnais. A little person sorcerer, with his face painted bright yellow, declares Laforgue a demon, and the two 'priests' encounter each other in a particularly memorable episode, 00:25:32 through 00:38:20.

➢ Influenced by the sorcerer and the other people, the escort party abandons 'Black Robe' and Daniel, the other Frenchman, to their fate. Daniel, in love with the chief's daughter, goes after them, and Black Robe prepares to fend for himself. Feeling guilty that they have abandoned him, a few of the party, including the chief and his family, return—only to be captured by a band of Iroquois raiders, 00:48:17 through 00:55:30.

➢ The natives and the Frenchmen are subjected to horrific tortures by the Iroquois, and the chief's young son is killed before his eyes. Black Robe's finger is cut off, and even more violence seems certain to follow, 01:04:18 through 01:09:40.

➢ Laforgue and the others escape, but he goes on alone, still hoping to find the mission to the Hurons. There he discovers only an old, dispirited priest, who, together with his associates, had been blamed for a bout of disease in the region. A group of Hurons tentatively approach Laforgue, asking him, 'Do you love us, Black Robe?' When he replies that he does, the leaders agree to be baptized. This culminating scene, between 01:24:02 and 01:37:05, is followed by the simple observation that this group will be massacred by the Iroquois 15 years later (in 1649).

## Discussion Questions

1.    Does the film suggest that the indigenous peoples were more brutal than the Europeans?

2.    What drives Black Robe? Does he ever have doubts?

3.    Is Black Robe so different from the religious officials among the natives?

## Further Reading and Viewing

A fascinating collection of documents concerning the *Jesuit Relations* and the images that were made to accompany them and other reports can be found in Allan Greer's *The Jesuit Relations: Natives and Missionaries in Seventeenth-Century North America* (Bedford/St. Martin's, 2000).

# *The Mission*

## Film Data

Year: 1986
Director: Roland Joffé
Screenplay: Robert Bolt
Music: Ennio Morricone
Length: 125 minutes
Rating: PG

## Connection to *Patterns of World History* & *Patterns of World History, Brief Edition*

Chapter 18: *New Patterns in New Worlds*

## Preview

*The Mission* is already a standard film for presentation, discussion, and application in world history courses, since it illuminates themes of cultural contact and rejection, racial chauvinism and enslavement, and religious violence and compassion. The film explores the consequences of a 1750 treaty between Spain and Portugal over their borderlands in South America, and specifically for the upland Guaraní people and the Jesuit missionaries who live among them. The Jesuits occupy a border zone themselves, as Europeans who reject the necessity of settling a quarrel between two European monarchs—and defy their superiors in the Church—in favor of the interests of the indigenous population. The film ends in an impressive and unforgettable battle scene that draws attention to the tragedies that continue to unfold in South America and every other region dealing with the legacies of Western colonization.

The British director Joffé had recently completed work on his piercing portrait of Pol Pot's Cambodia in *The Killing Fields* (1984) and had become aware, as had many in the early 1980s, of the bravery of Latin American Catholic priests. Inspired by a theology that married principles of social justice with the imperative to 'love thy neighbor', nuns and priests like Archbishop Óscar Romero of El Salvador had been murdered by oppressive regimes, some of them backed by an anti-Communist American government. Joffé seems to have become intrigued by the roots of these conflicts, which appeared to stem from the colonial period, during which Spanish, Portuguese, and other interests trumped those of the indigenous peoples and set up class systems based on ethnic origin.

The film also underscores the ongoing slave trade in South America, even after Spain had officially abolished it, and it demonstrates the dehumanizing attitudes of all the colonial powers in the region. Music emerges as a major force in the film, as the indigenous peoples living at the San Miguel Mission become famous for making violins and for performing contemporary European music. Ennio Morricone, who was famous for scoring Pontecorvo's *The Battle of Algiers* (see below), provided a similarly moving soundtrack for this film, melding together European and native South American rhythms and languages into an emotionally stirring whole. A visiting cardinal asks how someone could believe that an indigenous person does not have a soul when he can sing so beautifully, but he receives a dismissive rejoinder from the European authorities.

In photographing *The Mission*, the filmmakers took full advantage of the breathtaking natural environment of interior South America. The film was shot on location in Colombia, and the 'extras' were vital to its success. A documentary shot simultaneously with the film (and included on the 2003 DVD) centered on the experiences of these extras, most of whom were unclear about what precisely was involved in filmmaking and came to distrust the intentions and good faith of Joffé and his crew. To facilitate production of the film, the entire populations of four isolated villages were transported across the country for a period of several months. The extras' fees were intended to be distributed among the Waunana people, but the documentary demonstrates that the wounds of ethnic hatred and violence were still felt, over 200 years after the story told in *The Mission*.

## Recommended Scenes

➢ After the murder of a Jesuit priest by the Guaraní, Father Gabriel (played by Jeremy Irons) goes up to them to restart the mission. He uses his oboe to attract their interest, and he is hesitantly welcomed into their group, between 00:10:13 and 00:17:05.

➢ Cardinal Altamirano, himself a former Jesuit, comes to the region to mediate a dispute between Spanish and Portuguese authorities over the uplands that border their territories. Gabriel and his priests in the missions speak of the humanity of the Guaraní and insist to the Cardinal that the slave trade will be conducted more openly should the Portuguese be awarded the disputed land, 00:54:37 through 01:02:25.

➤ Even though he is dazzled by the success of Father Gabriel's mission, the Cardinal decides to side with the Portuguese to protect the interests of the Church in Europe, 01:18:58 through 01:26:15.

➤ Lent military support and expertise by the priest Rodrigo Mendoza (Robert De Niro), a former slaver and renegade, the Guaraní prepare for a violent confrontation with Portuguese soldiers. Father Gabriel prepares the noncombatants in his own way in the mission church, and, in the remainder of the film, the murder and forcible removal of the Guaraní and the priests unfolds. This simple but harrowing series of scenes is between 01:42:20 and 02:01:15.

## Discussion Questions

1.     Why do the Spanish and Portuguese colonial authorities collude in their attack on the Guaraní?

2.     Why does Cardinal Altamirano bend to the will of the colonists?

3.     What role does music play in the film as a whole?

## Further Reading and Viewing

Appeals on behalf of the surviving Guaraní people can be found at http://www.guarani-survival.org/ and (in French) http://www.unavenirpourlesguaranis.org/.

# *Jefferson in Paris*

## Film Data

Year: 1995
Director: James Ivory
Screenplay: Ruth Prawer Jhabvala
Music: Richard Robbins
Length: 139 minutes
Rating: PG-13

## Connection to *Patterns of World History* & *Patterns of World History, Brief Edition*

Chapter 19: *African Kingdoms, the Atlantic Slave Trade, and the Origins of Black America*

## Preview

While *Jefferson in Paris* is one of the less remarkable Merchant–Ivory films, it raises one of the most significant paradoxes in Western, as well as in US, history. As Samuel Johnson famously asked in 1775, 'How is it that we hear the loudest yelps for liberty among the drivers of Negroes?' Particularly in the 1990s, when DNA evidence confirmed what was long suspected, the hypocrisy of Thomas Jefferson—who declared that 'all men are created equal' while fathering a series of children with a woman whose body he owned—seemed an ideal subject for dramatization.

However, this film version adds further layers of complexity and irony by focusing on the period (1785–1789) in which Jefferson was the ambassador of the newly independent American states to the court of Louis XVI. Resident in Paris just before calls for 'Liberty, Equality, Fraternity!' capsized the French monarchy, Jefferson had brought with him his elder daughter Patsy and, eventually, his younger daughter Polly and her enslaved nurse, Sally Hemings. Sally and her brother James were in a unique position in Jefferson's Paris household, because they could, theoretically, have escaped Jefferson's control, as a petition process was available for the slave 'property' of foreign nationals. Because it was almost certainly in this period that Jefferson's 'relationship' with Sally began, it was also an intriguing question to consider the extent to which Sally 'consented' to the advances of her master and what promises might have been made on that occasion.

The film also introduces the figure of Maria Cosway, a white—and married—British woman with whom Jefferson must have had an affair in this period, judging from their correspondence. Because he had promised his wife on her deathbed that he would not remarry, Jefferson never sought another woman's hand in marriage, but neither did he deprive himself of female companionship altogether. The film implies that Mrs. Cosway ultimately came to be revolted by the moral horror of Jefferson's slave system and that Jefferson accordingly concentrated his attentions on the vulnerable young woman in his household. Although no more than 15 years old at the time and thus much younger than her 55-year-old master, Sally produced six children for Jefferson, all of whom he *owned* until they turned 21.

*Jefferson in Paris* does not shy away from the final, and perhaps the most revealing, irony of all, that Sally Hemings was almost certainly the half-sister of Jefferson's deceased wife. Jefferson's father-in-law had impregnated his slave, and the resulting child was 'given', together with other bridal property, to Jefferson when he married Martha Wayles Skelton. Such situations were not at all uncommon among slave-owning aristocrats in the southern states, and yet the film could have been more direct in identifying Jefferson's relationship with Sally Hemings as what it clearly was: coercive rape. Hemings had no choice but to yield to the whims of her master, and her children were used as leverage to keep her under his control. This image is certainly difficult to reconcile with the traditional one concerning 'The Sage of Monticello'.

Although Jefferson's white descendants were generally opposed to the notion that Jefferson also had African-American descendants, the scientific evidence of the relationship has been declared conclusive. It was perhaps a wise idea to entrust Jefferson's story to an Indian screenwriter whose family had escaped Nazi Germany, and not to an American, who might have been biased in respect to the talismanic effect of Jefferson's name. The result is not perfect, but several ideas of significance are raised in the film, touching on aspects of the Revolutionary period and beyond.

## Recommended Scenes

➢ Jefferson's slave James Hemings, whom he has brought to Paris, meets with French servants and is told that 'People get paid here'. Jefferson himself is a bona-fide celebrity in the city, and yet he witnesses the gathering storm as desperately poor people riot for bread in Parisian streets, 00:14:44 through 00:18:37.

➢ Jefferson (played—rather incongruously—by Nick Nolte) is confronted by French intellectuals with the obvious contradiction of a slave owner's having written, 'All men are created equal'. Jefferson's attractions for Mrs. Cosway grow, and the witticisms of the Versailles court enmesh him further into the delights of Paris, 00:22:26 through 00:29:55.

➢ The Marquis de Lafayette, who had played such a significant role in securing American independence, talks about the Revolution with Jefferson. He and other French veterans of this war—who had lost limbs in the service of the independence cause and had been promised some amount of financial compensation for their losses—confront Jefferson with the broken promises made by his compatriots in America, 00:36:42 through 00:40:19.

➢ Sally Hemings and her relationship to the deceased Mrs. Jefferson are introduced between 01:06:00 and 01:09:27.

➢ Dr. Guillotin demonstrates a model of his new machine to a group of delighted (if hopelessly naïve) aristocrats, and Jefferson decides to start paying Sally for her work, at least while they are in France, 01:29:24 through 01:36:18. The film strongly implies that Jefferson has already begun having sex with Sally.

➢ In the film's pivotal scene, between 02:03:19 and 02:15:45, Sally reveals to her brother James that she is pregnant, and James confronts the master. James' nagging resentment bubbles to the surface, and Sally miserably realizes her dependence on Jefferson and the Monticello system. To defuse the situation, Jefferson takes a 'solemn oath' that he will free Sally's children when they reach legal age and that he will free James soon after they return to Virginia.

## Discussion Questions

1.      Does the film excuse Jefferson's behavior and attitude in any way?

2.      How does the film explore the psychological dimensions of control in a slave system?

3.      What might the filmmakers be saying about the contemporary United States, by means of this portrait of a quintessential American?

## Further Reading and Viewing

One should view as many Merchant–Ivory films as possible, given their sumptuous look and sophisticated, thoughtful screenplays, but there are also several books that address the themes introduced in *Jefferson in Paris*. Annette Gordon-Reed's *Thomas Jefferson and Sally Hemings: An American Controversy* (University of Virginia Press, 1997) is the strongest and most compelling statement yet of the full consequences of the Hemings revelations, and her conclusions have been reinforced and developed by Henry Wiencek in his polemical *Thomas Jefferson and His Slaves* (Farrar, Straus and Giroux, 2012).

For Jefferson's own disturbing and difficult-to-take pronouncements on race and slavery, see David Waldstreicher's collected volume of *Notes on the State of Virginia, by Thomas Jefferson, with Related Documents* (Bedford/St. Martin's, 2002).

# *Jodhaa Akbar*

## Film Data

Year: 2008
Director: Ashutosh Gowariker
Screenplay: Ashutosh Gowariker and Haidar Ali
Lyrics and Music: Javed Akhtar and A. R. Rahman
Length: 209 minutes
Rating: No rating

## Connection to *Patterns of World History* & *Patterns of World History, Brief Edition*

Chapter 20: *The Mughal Empire: Muslim Rulers and Hindu Subjects*

## Preview

This exhilarating product of the Indian film industry is an old-fashioned historical epic that still manages to speak to contemporary concerns. The title character is a Hindu princess who married the Mughal Emperor Jalal ud-Din Muhammad Akbar, the Muslim ruler of Hindustan between 1556 and 1605. Akbar took Hindustan to its zenith of power and sophistication and was especially famous for his attempts to syncretize the many faith traditions of the subcontinent, replacing religious war with religious tolerance. His selection of a Hindu empress reflected his larger policies of acceptance and the rejection of religious dogmatism, and the film focuses on the evolution of Jodhaa's relationship with Jalal, from one of political convenience to full and intense romantic love.

*Jodhaa Akbar* demonstrates the justice of Jalal's claims to having been 'Akbar' ('the Great'), specifically in respect to his merciful treatment of enemies and his demonstrated respect for the adherents to other religions. In the film's climactic dance sequences—true to the conventions of 'Bollywood' cinema, the characters often break into song—Jalal's people express their respect for him and their delight in living in a Hindustan that is not pulling itself apart over religious difference. The historical Akbar experienced several setbacks in his policy of religious acceptance, as his syncretized faith of *din-i-ilahi* (divine faith) failed to convince many Muslims or Hindus and as his policies led some Muslims to doubt the sincerity of his commitment to Islam. Nevertheless, his attempt to reconcile different faith traditions has obvious resonance in India, a country that is majority Hindu but contains a significant Muslim minority.

Akbar's vision of a united country that would impose no special economic or social penalties on religious minorities is certainly an attractive one, even if it failed to be fully implemented in the sixteenth century and beyond. Gowariker's script, the uplifting music of A. R. Rahman, and the acting talents of two beautiful actors, Aishwarya Rai and Hrithik Roshan, in the lead roles add further attractions to the tale. Surprisingly, the film generated controversy in India, though merely in respect to the precise name of the princess who married Jalal. Regardless of the controversy, the sumptuous look and sound of *Jodhaa Akbar*, married to its wider meaning, merit the film's viewing by a global audience.

## Recommended Scenes

➤ A voiceover introduces the situation of Hindustan in 1555 together with brief sketches of the lives of Jalal ud-Din and Jodhaa as children, 00:02:51 through 00:07:33.

➤ The mature Jalal is introduced, and his policy of forgiving enemies on the battlefield is dramatically exemplified, 00:12:56 through 00:20:52.

➤ Jalal defies the expectations of his advisors by accepting the hand of a Hindu princess in marriage. Jodhaa is confronted with the news of her impending marriage and is told to marry for the sake of peace and her country's people, between 00:38:50 and 00:41:55.

➤ In their first encounter, Jodhaa boldly establishes conditions for the marriage, insisting that she be allowed to retain her faith and practice her customary rituals after the wedding. Jalal agrees to her conditions, and the wedding proceeds in a lively fashion—accompanied by Sufi singing and dancing—between 00:47:56 and 00:55:05.

➤ Experiencing the resistance of his more bigoted advisors, Jalal hears the sounds of his wife's singing in her private shrine and goes to offer his respects, 01:14:34 through 01:21:10.

➤ [The remaining scenes are found on the second disc, with times beginning again:]

➢ Walking among his subjects in disguise, Jalal hears of the special tax imposed on Hindus who wish to make a pilgrimage to their holy sites. Outraged by this unfair treatment, the Emperor abolishes the tax, and his people, overjoyed by his policy of tolerance, accord him the title 'Akbar' and sing and dance in his honor, 00:25:08 through 00:39:53.

➢ After triumphing over his rebellious brother-in-law and other enemies, Akbar reiterates his commitment to religious tolerance and predicts that mutual respect between Muslims and Hindus will make Hindustan a great country, 01:19:41 through 01:23:47.

## Discussion Questions

1.    Does the romantic story overwhelm or accentuate the themes of religious tolerance raised by the film?

2.    What indications does the film give of Jalal's essential decency and curiosity about other religious faiths?

3.    What forces are opposed to Jalal's vision of a united Hindustan, and why?

## Further Reading and Viewing

The policies and experiences of Akbar are profiled in M. Athar Ali's *Mughal India: Studies in Polity, Ideas, Society and Culture* (Oxford University Press, 2006).

# *The 47 Ronin*

## Film Data

Year: 1941–1942
Director: Kenji Mizoguchi
Based on the story by Seika Mayama
Screenplay: Kenichiro Hara and Yoshikata Yoda
Length: 222 minutes
Rating: No rating

## Connection to *Patterns of World History* & *Patterns of World History, Brief Edition*

Chapter 21: *Regulating the "Inner" and "Outer" Domains: China and Japan*

## Preview

The legend of the 'Forty-Seven Ronin' is appropriately described in terms of 'hothousing Japaneseness', as it is one of the central cultural components of modern Japan. While it is based on a series of historical incidents that took place in the Tokugawa Shogunate between 1701 and 1703, the story is probably more interesting for the various forms it has taken in the nineteenth and twentieth centuries. (And even in the twenty-first, as a new production, starring Keanu Reeves as the Ronin leader Oishi, is set for release in 2013.) Because the story hinges on the application of *bushido* and on the avenging of a former leader even to the point of one's own death, it has seemed to reflect the quintessence of the Japanese ideal of self-sacrifice and loyalty to one's superiors. As such, it has been put to propagandistic use, as in the present film, which was released a few weeks before Japanese bombers attacked Pearl Harbor in 1941.

The story began, as in this film version, with a knife attack by the *daimyo* (feudal lord) Asano Naganori on an imperial official named Kira Yoshinaka. Whatever the justice of the provocation, Asano had committed a serious breach in conduct and was forced to pay the most severe penalty. Even though Kira had suffered only a minor wound to his face, Asano was commanded to commit *seppuku*, ritual suicide. When he did so, his 47 samurai vassals were left leaderless ('*ronin*'), but they swore to avenge Asano's memory by killing Kira. Realizing they could not immediately exact their revenge on a vigilant Kira, the Ronin, led by Oishi Yoshio, blended into the wider society, biding their time for the exact moment when they would avoid detection. Kira heard of their going underground and let down his guard. Two years later, in January 1703, the 47 Ronin entered his home, chasing him and killing several of his retainers and wounding others, including Kira's grandson. When they finally trapped and overcame Kira, the Ronin cut off his head and brought it to their master's grave. However, they then decided to turn themselves into the authorities and killed themselves on one day that March, true to their code until the bitter end.

The story became popular in Japan in the Meiji period, after 1867, and was then transferred via A. B. Mitford's *Tales of Old Japan* (1871) to the West. To stoke morale and revive the *bushido* code for the twentieth century, the Japanese military commissioned a film version of the tale, and its first part was released in late 1941. While both the public and the government found the film boring and longwinded, a second part, detailing the murder of Kira (not depicted on screen) and the *seppuku* of the warriors, appeared the next year. Even though it is not a compelling film, it reflects the potential of a filmed legend to instill new notions of honor and self-sacrifice.

## Recommended Scenes

➤ The film opens with Asano's assault on Kira and his declaration that his only regret was that Kira was still alive, 00:06:57 through 00:12:26.

➤ Word arrives to the 47 samurai that their master has committed suicide, and his final *haiku* is read out to them, 00:39:21 through 00:43:15. After debating the most effective strategy to avenge Asano, the Ronin sign their names in blood to a document swearing vengeance, 01:07:08 through 01:17:11.

➤ Further preparations are made, and the head of Kira is brought to Asano's tomb, 02:48:05 through 02:55:37. Neither the invasion of Kira's home nor the appearance of dereliction by the Ronin is depicted.

➤ After the Ronin have turned themselves in and judgment has been passed against them, the Ronin prepare themselves for death with singing and music, 03:27:02 through 03:33:11.

> One at a time, each warrior goes behind a curtain to kill himself, and Oishi goes confidently to his death as music soars over the scene, 03:38:42 through 03:41:58.

## Discussion Questions

1.    What explanation does the film give for Asano's original outrage against Kira?

2.    What elements of the traditional narrative are omitted from this telling, and why?

3.    Would the film have had a propagandistic value in imperial wartime Japan?

## Further Reading and Viewing

Mitford's classic rendering of the Forty-Seven Ronin narrative is available online and in a number of illustrated editions. A more recent retelling of the story can be found in John Allyn's *The Forty-Seven Ronin Story* (Tuttle Publishing, 2006 revised edition).

# *Danton*

## Film Data

Year: 1983
Director: Andrzej Wajda
Screenplay: Jean-Claude Carrière
Based on the play by Stanisława Przybyzszewska
Music: Jean Prodomides
Length: 136 minutes
Rating: PG

## Connection to *Patterns of World History* & *Patterns of World History, Brief Edition*

Chapter 22: *Nation-States and Patterns of Culture in Europe and North America*

## Preview

The product of a unique collaboration between Western and Eastern Europeans, *Danton* is both a historical investigation of a transformational moment in Western civilization and an artifact of the waning Cold War of the early 1980s. While many saw connections between the French Revolution's spinning out of control in 1794 and the suppression of the Solidarity movement in Poland in 1981–1982, Wajda claimed that he had originally found inspiration for the film in a 1932 Polish play on Danton's life and execution. Since the French Revolution was generally viewed in the USSR and Warsaw Pact countries as an inspiration for the Bolshevik Revolution, contemporary statements could be made through comparisons to the major figures of the period. For example, Lenin might be compared to Robespierre, and the means by which they fomented and directed revolution—together with their resort to violence in the name of ideological purity—could be contrasted … albeit cautiously.

When Wajda set about the process of adapting the play to film, he was stymied by the imposition of martial law in Poland in December 1981. Because the generals had forbidden assemblies—and had defined an assembly as any gathering of more than four persons—it appeared impossible to make a film in his country. Undeterred in his ambition to film Danton's story, Wajda contacted the French screenwriter Jean-Claude Carrière and sought funding and suitable actors in France. When he landed Gérard Depardieu for the title role, the money began to flow, and he was allowed to film in the Place de la Concorde (the former Place de la Révolution and the site of the guillotines during the Terror) and—to his great surprise and relief—in the Assemblée Nationale itself.

Wajda managed to overcome another challenge in casting the principal roles in the film. Because he was determined to use a Polish actor, Wojciech Pszoniak, as Robespierre, most of the actors who interacted with him were speaking Polish and their words were dubbed into French. French actors were employed for the scenes involving Danton, and there was only one scene when Pszoniak and Depardieu appeared in the same space, each speaking his own language and with dubbing inserted afterward. Nevertheless, this scene is one of the film's best, and one of Depardieu's improvisations in rehearsal created a memorable encounter.

Many critics around the world saw in Depardieu's ebullient, earthy, and life-loving Danton a reflection of the heroic leader of the Solidarity movement, Lech Wałesa. While Wajda disavowed this connection, it is difficult to avoid, although Wałesa would eventually become President of Poland and not be executed by General Jaruzelski/Robespierre. Danton is a man of appetites, who eats, shouts, and touches actual people, while Robespierre merely orates about popular rights and sovereignty. Wajda believed that the message of *Danton*, promoting human rights and flexibility in reaction to ideological purity, was a significant one in the 1980s and beyond, and he was gratified that the film was re-released in 1989. This year marked not only the bicentennial of the storming of the Bastille, but also the beginning of the end for Communist domination of Eastern Europe.

## Recommended Scenes

➢ The film begins with a note that it takes place in Paris in spring 1794, or 'Year II of the Republic'. A child in Robespierre's household is prompted to recite from the Declaration of the Rights of Man and the Citizen, compiled 5 years earlier for a very different context, 00:02:51 through 00:10:28.

➢ News is received that the Committees of Security and Public Safety have shut down Danton's press mouthpiece and smashed their machines, between 00:26:30 and 00:30:58. Danton remains calm and cheers up his associates, especially Camille and Lucile Desmoulins.

➢ Danton invites Robespierre to his home and confronts him in a blistering encounter, 00:39:24 through 00:48:02. Declaring he would rather be guillotined than a guillotiner, Danton places Robespierre's hands around his neck so he can see what it feels like actually to kill someone.

➢ Danton and his comrades are arrested, but he is still the people's favorite, 01:28:35 through 01:32:15.

➢ Robespierre poses for his portrait in the studio of the artist Jacques-Louis David, 01:40:38 through 01:45:45. Notice particularly the sketches from his painting of the Tennis Court Oath (from which Robespierre suggests that some people be removed, à la Stalin's photographs) and the ongoing work on *The Death of Marat*. Marat had been killed in July 1793 in his bath, and the scene suggests that even more violence is soon to follow.

➢ The culminating moment of the film is reached when the various stages of the guillotining of Danton are depicted, 02:00:02 through 02:13:50. This is one of the few filmed—and realistic—sequences showing the elements of execution by guillotine, and blood drips from the blade as disturbing music plays over the scene. The film ends with the same boy from the film's opening reciting again from the Declaration of the Rights of Man. The words now seem to have a bitter and ironic meaning.

## Discussion Questions

1.    How does the film deal with the issue of press freedom?

2.    Who spoke for 'the people' during the Revolution?

3.    How does the film warn about the dangers of ideological purity?

## Further Reading and Viewing

The 2009 Criterion Collection release of *Danton* contains a documentary on the making of the film and focuses particularly on responses to it by Poles. A compelling biography of Maximilien Robespierre can be found in Ruth Scurr's aptly titled *Fatal Purity: Robespierre and the French Revolution* (Chatto & Windus, 2006).

# *Angels and Insects*

## Film Data

Year: 1995
Director: Philip Haas
Screenplay by Philip Haas and Belinda Haas
Based on the novella *Morpho Eugenia*, by A. S. Byatt
Costume Designer: Paul Brown
Music: Alexander Balanescu
Length: 118 minutes
Rating: R

## Connection to *Patterns of World History* & *Patterns of World History, Brief Edition*

Chapter 23: *Industrialization and Its Discontents*

## Preview

Best known for her novel *Possession* (1990), which followed scholars of Victorian literature in their investigation of a long-buried relationship, A. S. Byatt returned to the mid-Victorian period in her short but ambitious novella *Morpho Eugenia* (1992). Byatt's fiction often hinges on the intellectual excitement of delving into the past, and this novel tackles a very large subject: the earth-shattering challenges posed, particularly to religious and ethical thought, by the scientific advances of Charles Darwin. Rather than detailing Darwin's life, or those of any actual people in the Britain of his era, Byatt constructs a story set on a fictional estate in the early 1860s, just after the publication of Darwin's *On the Origin of Species* (1859).

Her central character, William Adamson (the names in the novel are all evocative), hails from a part of Yorkshire that 'consisted of foul black places amongst fields and rough land of great beauty' and, in his boyhood, was drawn to collecting samples of plants and insects in those fields and then studying them. Emerging from this cocoon as a professional naturalist, Adamson was transplanted to the Amazon basin, where he collected more samples and made further investigations of a habitat teeming with life. Returning to

England, he was shipwrecked and spent 15 harrowing days on a lifeboat in the Atlantic. As the novella opens, in 1860, he has been invited to stay at the home of Harald Alabaster, charged with organizing and classifying an impressive collection of plant and animal samples Alabaster has acquired over several years.

Over the course of the novel, Adamson is brought into the circle of Alabaster's family, forms a close working relationship with the younger children's governess, Matilda (Matty) Crompton, composes a book about the insect life on the Alabaster estate entitled *The Swarming City* … and makes a shocking and horrible discovery toward the end of the story. *Morpho Eugenia* is thus a traditional piece of fiction, though one that engages, in a profound and thoughtful way, with the intellectual tidal wave that came crashing upon sedate Victorians in the form of 'evolution by means of natural selection'. The highlights of the novel involve Adamson's conversations with Lord Alabaster, who has taken holy orders in the Church of England and is deeply troubled about the full implications of Darwin's theory, which seems to call God's existence into doubt. Adamson speaks with confidence about the rationality and scientific acumen of Darwin's investigations, but his confidence in scientific progress is badly shaken when he discovers a strange and 'unnatural' relationship in his own household.

The filmed version of this rich and complex story is particularly remarkable for its use of color and a complex visual palette. The costumes of the women, in particular, are deliberately designed to mirror the insects that Adamson and his associates are studying. By these means, the so-called 'angels' of the mid-Victorian home can literally be viewed as 'insects', following their instincts in maintaining the needs of themselves and their 'hive'. In her drab, austere clothes that are so different from the brilliant gowns of Eugenia Alabaster, Kristin Scott Thomas, as Matty Crompton, manages to stay invisible to Adamson until the final scenes. The two scientists escape Bredely Hall to further researches in South America, and perhaps they will eventually find themselves on Darwin's famous Galapagos Islands?

## Recommended Scenes

➤ The opening credits profile the exuberant dances and mating rituals Adamson had encountered in the Amazon, and the scene dissolves to its European equivalent, a ball in progress on an English estate, 00:00:05 through 00:07:20.

➤ In a dinnertime conversation, Adamson and Lord Alabaster (joined by Miss Crompton) discuss Mr. Darwin's theories about why the male of the species is often so much more adorned and elaborate in his coloring than the female, 00:11:30 through 00:16:39. Eugenia, the most beautiful and eligible of Alabaster's many daughters, later appears in a fantastic bee-like costume, and she asks Adamson about life among the 'savages'.

➤ Adamson takes Miss Crompton and her young charges on nature 'rambles' on the estate, and he leaps high in the social order by convincing Eugenia to marry him. Nevertheless, as he is often reminded by his frequently drunk and invariably belligerent brother-in-law Edgar, he is 'not one of us', and it becomes clear that his sole purpose is to squire more squires on Eugenia.

➤ In the meantime, Adamson throws himself into his close observations of insect life on the grounds of the Hall, discovering Matty's drawing ability and discovering in her the intellectual stimulation that he lacks in his wife, 00:51:53 through 00:56:50.

➤ In the crucial scenes of the film, 01:11:20 through 01:21:22, William and Matty discover a 'slaving raid' by one group of ants against another, and they, naturally, discuss the ongoing Civil War in the United States. (One is reminded of Thoreau's 'Battle of the Ants' in *Walden* (1854).) Their anthropomorphic descriptions of the raid's progress are followed by a rich and wide-ranging discussion between Adamson and Harald about God and nature post-Darwin.

➤ William discovers a shocking secret that everyone else in the household, including Matty, apparently already knows, and a new, more intimate relationship springs up between William and Matty, 01:37:31 through 01:50:50.

## Discussion Questions

1.    How does the film compare the mores of 'civilized' people in England with those of the 'savages' elsewhere?

2.    How and why does the film compare human and insect life?

3.    How does Darwinian theory undermine Lord Alabaster's faith in God?

## Further Reading and Viewing

A superb communal biography of the many prominent individuals who began to question and lose their Christian faith in the nineteenth century can be found in A. N. Wilson's *God's Funeral: The Decline of Faith in Western Civilization* (W.W. Norton, 1999). The title of the book is borrowed from a poem by Thomas Hardy in which God is literally carried to his grave by mourners who wonder what, if anything, will replace their deity. The impact of Darwinian thought, in particular, recurs throughout this book.

# *Tai-Pan*

## Film Data

Year: 1986
Director: Daryl Duke
Based on the novel by James Clavell
Music: Maurice Jarre
Length: 127 minutes
Rating: R

## Connection to *Patterns of World History* & *Patterns of World History, Brief Edition*

Chapter 24: *The Challenge of Modernity, East Asia*

## Preview

James Clavell's 1966 novel dramatizes the experiences of British merchants in Canton (Guangzhou) in the aftermath of the First Opium War (1839–1842) and the circumstances surrounding the foundation of Hong Kong as a British outpost. Unfortunately, it also romanticizes the life of a Scottish opium dealer and his family, while minimizing the views of the Chinese on this trade war, which would have enormous ramifications for China and the globe into the next century. The 'Tai-Pan' or 'Supreme Leader' is, like a present-day pirate, perpetually skirting the law and often on the verge of bankruptcy. Nevertheless, he manages to establish his position and solidify the standing of his business, (ironically?) called 'Noble House', in the midst of a fluid and dangerous situation.

The film version of this novel, made with the cooperation of the Chinese, Macau, and Hong Kong governments, is unimaginative and tainted by a pervasive sense of the childishness and barbarity of the Chinese people. On the other hand, in this regard it demonstrates some of the attitudes of the nineteenth century and the determination of Westerners to establish a trading foothold in East Asian ports, a story that is continuing to unfold into our own time. Chinese characters in the film often refer to the British as 'the barbarians', who serve 'a barbarian Queen', have corrupted their society with opium, and have little regard for the noble and dignified people they have encountered.

At the heart of the film is the relationship between the Tai-Pan, Dirk Struan, and his Chinese mistress, May-May [sic]. This relationship covers the gamut from comedy to tragedy, and, while their mutual love is demonstrated repeatedly, it is accompanied by scenes of humiliation and degradation for May-May, whose only goal is to hold onto her handsome Western lover. The film also prefigures the handover of Hong Kong to the People's Republic of China, which was accomplished, after the expiration of a 99-year lease, in June 1997, and it concludes over a wide-angle shot of Hong Kong's modern harbor, the legacy of the Tai-Pan for today's world.

## Recommended Scenes

➤ An effective opening image shows Chinese ships emerging from the mist over the Pearl River in 1839, 00:00:34 through 00:07:50. The imperial official Lin Zexu demands that the foreigners' opium, a poisonous substance for his people, be destroyed and their trade abandoned.

➤ Driven out of Canton, Struan discovers an uninhabited island at the river's mouth, and he is determined to claim it for Britain and in defiance of China's 'medieval monarch'. This land will eventually become Hong Kong, and its founding is detailed between 00:18:24 and 00:23:17.

➤ Struan describes his plans for Hong Kong to his reluctant son, and he also justifies the opium trade, as a means of securing tea for Britain, 01:08:15 through 01:12:30.

➤ Some of the more disturbing facets of Struan's relationship with May-May are shown between 01:26:03 through 01:29:22.

➤ Struan duels with his oldest enemy in the midst of a typhoon that is hitting Hong Kong, 01:48:45 through 01:54:53.

➤ Dirk's son finds him and his lover May-May dead, holding each other in their home, in the typhoon's aftermath. A final shot hovers over the modern harbor of Hong Kong, 01:59:50 through 02:05:25.

## Discussion Questions

1.    Does the film attempt to justify the opium trade and the British seizure of Hong Kong?

2.    Is the sexual relationship (bordering on the sadomasochistic) between Struan and May-May a subtle reference to the Western–Chinese relationship on a macro scale?

3.    Does the film hint that the Chinese were capable of resisting the mercantile imperialism of the British in this period?

## Further Reading and Viewing

Lin Zexu's impassioned 1839 letter to Queen Victoria, complaining about the opium trade and its effects on the Chinese people, can be found at: http://www.fordham.edu/halsall/mod/1839lin2.asp.

# *Battleship Potemkin*

## Film Data

Year: 1925
Director: Sergei Eisenstein
Cinematography: Eduard Tisse
Length: 69 minutes
Rating: No rating

## Connection to *Patterns of World History* & *Patterns of World History, Brief Edition*

Chapter 25: *Adaptation and Resistance: The Ottoman and Russian Empires*

## Preview

Eisenstein's masterful and enormously influential silent film helps to illustrate the failed revolutions of 1905 in Russia, as well as the lingering effects of that revolution in the 1910s, 1920s, and far beyond. In the midst of a humiliating war with Japan and in sympathy with protesters who had gone on strike and faced violent reprisals throughout the country, a group of sailors on a battleship near Odessa (on the Black Sea) mutinied against their commanders in June 1905. Because Vladimir Lenin had celebrated the heroism of those who had marched on the Tsar's Winter Palace and had been shot in a series of episodes on 'Bloody Sunday' in January 1905, the leaders of the new Soviet Union looked back on the events of that year with pride and enthusiasm. Eisenstein was commissioned to compose a film that would mark the twentieth anniversary of these events, and *Battleship Potemkin* was the first cinematic production to be presented at the famed Bolshoi Ballet in Moscow.

From its first showing in 1925, with veterans of the 1905 uprising in attendance, Eisenstein's film would be acclaimed in Russia and abroad as a masterpiece of its genre. The sequence detailing the massacre of civilians on the Odessa Steps became legendary in film history, and its searing images were considered, from the beginning, too intense for some viewers. In fact, the subsequent history of the film is an indicator of its power and the tangled legacies of a film made for an explicitly propagandistic purpose, in an age of propaganda.

After its showing in theaters throughout the USSR in 1925–1926, *Battleship Potemkin* was swiftly scheduled for release in Germany. Although Weimar Germany was renowned for its open-minded and generally tolerant culture, the film was drastically cut by censors, who feared that its images were too explicit and might incite revolutionary action. Because the Weimar government had been created in the aftermath of both the Great War and the failed Communist uprising in Berlin in 1918–1919, censors had an interest in shaving out elements that seemed tinged (literally) by the red flag of Bolshevism. Cuts made to the film at this point and in subsequent reconfigurations, in both Germany and the USSR, have created great difficulty in reconstructing what precisely Eisenstein had intended to be his final cut.

In 2005, German film restorers attempted to identify and reattach the severed images to Eisenstein's film, and the result of their painstaking work has been made available in a new DVD accompanied with freshly written music. The musical accompaniment was crucial to a film's success in the silent era, and this score is based on rhythms composed for the original German screening of the film. The DVD also restores one of the most remarkable visual elements of the film, the hand-painted red flag that is hoisted over the ship in Odessa's harbor, to the jubilation of the crowd.

## Recommended Scenes

➤ A group of sailors mutiny against their officers who, with the collusion of an Orthodox priest, are preparing to fire on them. Repeatedly appealing to their fellow soldiers as 'brothers', the mutineers succeed in taking over the battleship between 00:20:50 and 00:27:39.

➤ However, when the guiding spirit and leader of the rebellion is killed, his body is laid open to public view in Odessa's harbor front. Outraged by the death of the man, Odessa's citizens erupt into a spontaneous revolt against the local authorities, and the sailors hoist a red flag, 00:39:08 through 00:42:06.

➤ Odessan men, women, and children cheer the sailors on the steps leading down to the harbor, but then shots ring out and a panic ensues. In the film's most riveting scene, individuals are shot by the military and trampled to death on the steps, 00:45:28 through 00:52:29.

➤ The *Potemkin* goes into battle against naval forces, but the sailors on the other ships unexpectedly refuse to fire on their brothers, 01:01:47 through 01:08:05.

## Discussion Questions

1.    Does *Battleship Potemkin* adequately explain the source of the revolutions of 1905 or the governmental response?

2.    What is the significance of the Odessan mob's attack on an anti-Semitic commentator in the crowd?

3.    Joseph Goebbels lauded Eisenstein's film as a perfect example of modern propaganda techniques, and he encouraged Leni Riefenstahl (see below) to emulate Eisenstein. Is *Battleship Potemkin* a 'propaganda film'?

## Further Reading and Viewing

Neal Bascomb's *Red Mutiny: Eleven Fateful Days on the Battleship Potemkin* (Houghton Mifflin, 2007) reconstructs the specific events that accompanied the mutiny in June 1905. Moreover, a 1943 film entitled *Seeds of Freedom*, written by the (later blacklisted) writer Albert Maltz, centered on a fictional survivor of the *Potemkin* and his resistance to Nazi aggression during World War II.

# *Zulu*

## Film Data

Year: 1964
Director: Cy Endfield
Screenplay: John Prebble and Cy Endfield
Music: John Bury
Length: 138 minutes
Rating: No rating

## Connection to *Patterns of World History* & *Patterns of World History, Brief Edition*

Chapter 26: *The New Imperialism in the Nineteenth Century*

## Preview

*Zulu* is both a celebration of the 'heroism' of a small contingent of British troops who held off a Zulu army in January 1879 and a product of the era of European withdrawal from their colonial holdings. The story was inspired by a battle at Rorke's Drift in South Africa, just after a disastrous defeat for the British at Isandlwana, and it provides extensive portraits of the English and Welsh soldiers in this small frontier unit. Very little attention is given in the film to the Zulu warriors who were defending their homeland against European invasion, although the historical Chief Cetewayo of the Zulu makes a brief appearance early in the film.

It is critical to bear in mind the immediate context of this film. For one example, Kenya had been granted its independence by the British government in 1963, after the Mau Mau uprising had focused British attention throughout the 1950s—and, only in July 2012, the UK government admitted to having used torture and sexual abuse against rebels in the period. South Africa had imposed its draconian apartheid regime of racial segregation and subjugation of the majority Black population in 1948, and pressure would mount throughout the 1960s and 1970s for the British government and the British Commonwealth to make a stand against these and similar abuses in Rhodesia (today's Zimbabwe). It may seem counterintuitive to have made a movie about British soldiers at the early stages of the 'New Imperialism' within this significant moment of retrenchment from colonial hegemony. However, there may be a subtext in *Zulu*, offering respect and appreciation for the skills of the determined warriors who resisted colonial incursions … at least in the nineteenth century.

The film opens on the catastrophic (for the British) defeat at Isandlwana, one of the few instances in which colonial powers were turned back, if temporarily, by native troops. *Zulu* was made, as its end credits attest, with the cooperation of the current Zulu Chief Buthelezi, and it was filmed in Natal, employing Zulu extras. As per South Africa's apartheid laws, the extras could not be paid, but the filmmakers left behind animals and the implements from their sets, which may have been some compensation. The Boer War is also prefigured in the screenplay, with the appearance of a Boer farmer who advises the British—and who demonstrates the skillful and advanced tactics that had been developed by the Zulu army. The film presents the Zulu as merely the enemy, but the soldiers and other personnel at the fort often ask why this war is necessary. None of the questions receives a satisfactory answer, and that may have been the director's intention.

## Recommended Scenes

> The disaster at Isandlwana, in which roughly 1,500 British troops (and very likely many more Zulu) had been killed, is mentioned, and the scene opens on an exuberant Zulu celebration, attended by a Swedish missionary and his daughter. The customs of Europeans and Africans are compared, and Cetewayo makes a comment to the Reverend Witt, 00:01:35 through 00:13:02.

> Michael Caine, playing the upper-class and rather irritating commander Bromhead, is introduced, and it is clear that he will come to loggerheads with the fort's engineer Chard, 00:25:33 through 00:30:31.

> News arrives of the defeat at Isandlwana, together with further news of a coming attack by 4,000 Zulu warriors on the fort, which can muster only 100 British defenders. Reverend Witt delivers a pacifist message, and 40 native troops abandon the fort, 00:51:25 through 00:56:46.

➤ Zulu warriors appear on the ridge, and they beat their shields in sight of the fort, shouting their battle cry '*Usuthu!*' to terrify the defenders. This is an effective tactic, but the defenders fire volleys of guns at the first waves of Zulu attackers. The remainder continues chanting and massing for further attack, 01:05:55 through 01:13:10.

➤ Sniper units among the Zulu are shown, and the film moves repeatedly from the Zulu faces to British ones. A grievously wounded soldier asks the simple question, 'Why?', between 01:20:47 and 01:30:54.

➤ The culminating moment of the film displays a contingent of Welshmen (of course, given the Welsh reputation for choral singing) in full-throated hymn singing, designed to answer a song by the Zulu, 01:58:33 through 02:06:08. The British fire in ranks on the Zulu, and yet the native troops keep pressing on. The engagement ends with piles of Zulu corpses around the successfully defended fort.

➤ The few survivors are relieved, but they receive word that another massive group of Zulu are heading toward the fort. However, this group of Zulu begin singing because they are, they are told, 'saluting fellow braves' on the British side. The film ends by noting the Victoria Crosses that were given to the real men profiled throughout, 02:10:41 through 02:18:30.

## Discussion Questions

1.    Does the film glorify British militarism, at least in the nineteenth century?

2.    What role does Adendorff the Boer play in the film?

3.    Is Reverend Witt's pacifist message taken seriously?

## Further Reading and Viewing

A segment of the video series 'History's Turning Points', produced in 1995, profiles the Battle of Isandlwana, focusing in particular on the goals of Cetewayo and of Theophilus Shepstone, who presided over the annexation of the Transvaal in 1877 and ruled South Africa from Pretoria in this period.

# *Camila*

## Film Data

Year: 1984
Director: Maria Luisa Bemberg
Length: 105 minutes
Rating: R

## Connection to *Patterns of World History* & *Patterns of World History, Brief Edition*

Chapter 27: *Creoles and Caudillos: Latin America and the Caribbean in the Nineteenth Century*

## Preview

*Camila* wrenches the maximum emotional power from an actual doomed love affair that unfolded in 1840s Argentina, and it also obliquely comments on the current situation of the country in the 1980s. When Camila O'Gorman, an upper-class Buenos Aires woman, ran away with her lover, the Jesuit priest Ladislao Gutierrez, the entire society—and especially Argentina's dictator, Juán Manuel de Rosas—was outraged and determined to bring the miscreants to justice. The pair was detected in a rural section of the country, living under assumed identities and operating a school, and they were sentenced to death by firing squad upon their repatriation to the city. The imposition of this extremely severe penalty can make sense only given the immediate backdrop of the red-draped rule of 'The Governor', which is ever-present in the film.

Between 1829 and 1852, de Rosas combined control of the military with the collusion of the institutional Church and a cult of personality into a highly combustible formula that would re-emerge in the twentieth century. His portrait, invariably framed with red cloth, appeared in churches and private homes, and Argentinians were enjoined (or rather forced) to wear red ribbons, dresses, and vests as a mark of their loyalty to the regime. A 'Holy Federation' of government-sponsored thugs enforced conformity to de Rosas by patrolling the streets and murdering its opponents, whether real or imagined. In such a society, the scandalous affair between Camila and Ladislao was not merely a private matter. Because they represented the twin pillars of that society, the Buenos Aires aristocracy and the Catholic Church, the lovers' flouting of convention was answered with swift and brutal force.

By returning to this tragic love story, the Argentinian director Maria Luisa Bemberg was drawing clear parallels between the personal regime of de Rosas and the military dictatorship out of which her country had just emerged. Between 1976 and 1983, a military junta, ruling Argentina with an iron fist, appealed to the most extreme right-wing elements in the Church, provoked an unsuccessful war with the UK over the Falkland Islands, and inflicted horrendous violations of human rights on its own people in an episode known as the 'Dirty War'. *Camila* references de Rosas' opposition to British annexation of the Falklands (known to Argentinians as Las Malvinas), which parallels the 1982 Falklands War, and the sufferings of the '*desaparecidos*' (the 'disappeared') and their families in recent years are vividly recalled in this historical film. Random acts of murder are observed with horror and frustration, and Camila asks, 'When will it all end?' By casting her cinematic vision back nearly 150 years, Bemberg elicited sympathy for those who defy a regime touting the glories of 'law and order' as well as Christian purity.

## Recommended Scenes

➤ A vibrant, intellectually curious young woman, Camila encounters a handsome priest in a game of blind man's buff, and their attraction for each other is instantaneous and palpable, between 00:12:18 and 00:16:15.

➤ A Holy Federation contingent murders an inoffensive bookseller who is Camila's friend, 00:21:13 through 00:28:39.

➤ Camila confesses her love to Ladislao and learns that he reciprocates that love. Her face is framed in a diamond created by the grill of the confessional box, in an expressive scene between 00:38:06 and 00:41:04.

➤ The lovers run away together and make love in a carriage (in a scene reminiscent of one in Gustave Flaubert's *Madame Bovary*). The Governor sends out orders to have them arrested, and Camila's father, offended by her outrage against society, refuses to assist her, 00:53:56 through 01:02:30.

➢ The lovers spend an idyllic time teaching in the country, but, when their disguise is discovered by a visiting priest, they are returned to prison in Buenos Aires. They are both condemned to death, even though Camila is now pregnant with Ladislao's child, 01:14:36 through 01:24:51.

➢ Camila and Ladislao are tied to chairs and shot by a firing squad. Her last vision, before the blindfold is placed over her eyes, is of Ladislao between 01:36:30 and 01:42:20.

## Discussion Questions

1.    What is the emblematic significance of the blindfold throughout the film?

2.    What do the various attitudes of Camila's father and mother suggest about Buenos Aires society in the de Rosas period?

3.    How did de Rosas conflate '*libertinaje*' ('libertine behavior') with chaos and societal disorder?

## Further Reading and Viewing

The official post-regime government report on the fate of Argentina's 11,000 'Disappeared' can be read, in an English version, at: http://www.desaparecidos.org/nuncamas/web/english/library/nevagain/nevagain_000.htm.

# *Gallipoli*

## Film Data

Year: 1981
Director: Peter Weir
Screenplay: David Williamson
Based on a story by Peter Weir
Length: 111 minutes
Rating: PG

## Connection to *Patterns of World History* & *Patterns of World History, Brief Edition*

Chapter 28: *World War and Competing Visions of Modernity*

## Preview

According to the Australian director Peter Weir, the main story of *Gallipoli* was inspired by a spare comment contained in C. E. W. Bean's mammoth 12-volume *Official History of Australia in the War of 1914–1918*. Describing the heroic performance of a Western Australian regiment at the Battle of Gallipoli in the summer of 1915, Bean observed that one young man was last seen running toward enemy lines as if he were in a schoolboys' footrace instead of rushing into machine-gun fire. In collaboration with David Williamson, Weir crafted a profoundly moving script tracing the friendship of two soldiers from western Australia to training camp outside Cairo to the death of an 18-year-old man in a pointless military action directed by incompetent and intransigent commanders.

      With one third of the film devoted to the lives of Archie Hamilton and Frank Dunne in Australia and the second third highlighting the emotional depths of their friendship while exploring Egypt, the war appears only in the final section, accompanied by the strains of Remo Giazotto's wonderful neo-Baroque 'Adagio in G Minor'. *Gallipoli* underscores the wasteful and unnecessary loss of, particularly, soldiers from Australia and New Zealand, who were shoved over their trenches into enemy gunfire by callous British commanders. In this story, Frank runs as quickly as he can, carrying the orders that will countermand yet another futile assault. However, he arrives too late to prevent Archie's heroic race and death in battle. The camera freezes on the iconic image (captured for the film's poster) showing Archie at the moment he has been hit by bullets. Nevertheless the image also recalls the exhilaration with which he had crossed the finish line in a sprint back home.

The film is thus an indictment of the futility of all wars, and perhaps not only of this segment of 'The War That Will End War', in H. G. Wells' inimitable phrase. It also profiles the unique experiences of Australians, and particularly the children of the original pioneers to the remote stretches of the continent's west, as they encountered a wider global culture in the early twentieth century. *Gallipoli* contains characters drawn from various classes of Australian society, even including a brief cameo by the Aboriginal man who works for Archie's family, but the most telling comments probably come from a drifter who is unaware of the War and doubts whether it is important enough to warrant such a long journey.

## Recommended Scenes

➤ *Gallipoli* opens with the experiences and frustrations of an adolescent who runs like the wind but feels that he should, despite being under the official recruiting age, join the war effort, 00:10:20 through 00:16:30.

➤ Archie and his 'mate' Frank, a more cynical but ultimately convinced itinerant worker, decide to volunteer for a cavalry unit. Archie succeeds in being inducted, despite being too young, and Frank is sent into an infantry unit after his lack of riding prowess is demonstrated, between 00:36:35 and 00:45:53.

➤ Frank and his new mates are confronted by stuffy British officers and duplicitous local merchants near their training camp in Egypt, 00:55:40 through 01:01:40.

➤ Reunited at the training camp, Frank and Archie explore the pyramids, leaving graffiti on the monument as Napoleon's soldiers had in 1798, 01:08:37 through 01:13:40.

➤ The men are introduced to nighttime views of battle and to the incessant sound of shelling between 01:16:30 and 01:21:40.

➤ The film's final moments profile the soldiers' preparations before they go over their trench—in what they seem to realize is a doomed endeavor. Archie is killed just as Frank reaches the commander with orders countermanding the assault, 01:35:20 through 01:48:04.

## Discussion Questions

1.   Is this primarily a story of World War I or of Australians in World War I?

2.   How does the film compare the experiences of Turks and Australians in the course of the battle?

3.   How does *Gallipoli* deal with the connections between athletic prowess and military action?

## Further Reading and Viewing

There are several multivolume histories of the Great War (John Buchan's 24-volume work, published between 1915 and 1919, is one of the most remarkable), and students may be inspired to seek out similar stories from these records and to compose their own screenplays.

# *Triumph des Willens (Triumph of the Will)*

## Film Data

Year: 1935
Director: Leni Riefenstahl
Length: 110 minutes
Rating: No rating

## Connection to *Patterns of World History* & *Patterns of World History, Brief Edition*

Chapter 28: *World War and Competing Visions of Modernity*

## Preview

The official film of the Nazi Party's Nuremberg rally, held between September 4 and 10, 1934, *Triumph of the Will* is surely the most controversial film ever made, and it is the only one in this book that is itself a historical artifact. Because of this film and its propaganda effect, Riefenstahl was effectively shut out of the filmmaking world after 1945. Accused of being a collaborator with the Nazi regime, she was detained at various points in Allied custody and confronted with charges. However, she was ultimately released, proclaiming—as she would for the next six decades—that she was not personally responsible for the violence perpetrated by Nazi Germany.

Turning her artistic attentions to photography, Riefenstahl went on to document the lives of the Nuba people in the Sudan and would, in her 70s, 80s, and 90s, take her camera underwater, capturing wonderful images of marine wildlife and coral reefs. Whatever her subject matter, however, her work was condemned for its 'fascist aesthetic' which had been, according to her many critics, inculcated in the 1930s and carefully nurtured ever afterward. When she was interviewed for a 1993 documentary on her 'Wonderful, Horrible Life', Riefenstahl protested that she had produced an 'artistic film' and not a 'political film' in

*Triumph of the Will.* If the Nazi Party conference had been composed of 'vegetables or fruit' instead of political speeches, she would have been driven by the same overriding concern: to make the film as 'interesting' as possible.

Stage-managed by Albert Speer, the Nuremberg rally was captured by means of a series of innovative camera angles, and Riefenstahl even had her camera crew wear roller skates and install moving cameras on flagpoles in order to achieve dynamic shots at critical moments. Castigated for enhancing Hitler's image in the speeches that highlight the film, she, again in the 1993 documentary, averred that when an artist is filming a speech, whether its subject is 'trees, fish, or politics', it has to be trimmed to make it 'interesting'. Two-hour speeches had to be condensed to 5 minutes, and she claimed not to have cared about—or even much listened to—what Hitler was actually saying. The film constantly shifts from Hitler to the crowd and back again, stressing the solitary individual and his sway over exuberant, cheering masses.

Riefenstahl's artistic genius is generally acknowledged and her expert handling of many technical challenges resulted in international acclaim in Europe and North America in the late 1930s. She was particularly renowned for her ability to connect movement to music, and she observed that the editing process alone required 5 months' work, virtually around the clock. She remains, even after her death in 2003 at the age of 101, an extremely complex historical figure, and her artistic legacy continues to be reinterpreted and reassessed. Her achievement in the medium of film poses the question of the artist's moral responsibility for the effects of his or her creation, and whether the simple claim of 'not being political' is sufficient.

## Recommended Scenes

➢ A series of opening captions announces the date of the rally as being, for one example, 19 months after the beginning of the German '*Wiedergeburt*' ('Regeneration'). The captions dissolve into the mist, and Hitler's airplane descends through this mist over Nuremberg, 00:02:19 through 00:06:20.

➢ A night rally is held at Hitler's hotel, complete with torches, electric light bulbs, and floodlights, 00:11:09 through 00:14:02. The images are designed to recall the night of January 30, 1933, when Hitler was greeted as the new *Reichskanzler* with a torch-lit parade, prompting an observer to note that the Nazi government was '*der Sprung ins Dunkle*' ('a leap in the dark').

➤ One of the most frequently referenced elements of the film is the mass demonstration of the Reich Labor Service, between 00:34:17 and 00:41:18. The men in the unit hold and present their shovels exactly like rifles, and a worshipful young man calls upon each of his '*Kameraden*' to name their hometowns. The final one notes that he is from 'the Saar', which was of particular relevance in 1934.

➤ Hitler speaks before a rally of the Hitler Youth (*Hitler Jugend* or HJ), between 00:47:44 and 00:55:10. The camera moves along beside his platform and gazes up at him, as the audience is enjoined to do as well.

➤ Hitler, Himmler, and the new (after the violent removal of Ernst Röhm a few months earlier) and more malleable SA (*Sturmabteilung*) commander lay a wreath at a memorial to President Hindenburg, 01:05:07 through 01:16:43. The image of three figures strolling past assembled masses has been copied many times, from *Return of the Jedi* to *Gladiator*, and one of the moving cameras, attached to a flagpole, can be seen on its upward trajectory in this shot.

➤ Hitler offers his final speech of the rally, reminding the audience that the NSDAP (the Nazi Party) was once composed of only seven members and now it is composed of millions, 01:40:05 through 01:48:15. Hitler's distinctive style of speech, involving upward gazes, emphatic hand gestures, and accelerating passion, is captured effectively in this scene, and many of these elements would assist Charles Chaplin in his masterful parody of Hitler as 'Adenoid Hynkel' in *The Great Dictator* (1940).

## Discussion Questions

1. Does the film convey historical information, specifically about the inner workings of Hitler's government?

2. Is there a detectable theme in *Triumph of the Will*?

3. How are young people and youth culture incorporated into the film?

## Further Reading and Viewing

It is particularly valuable to watch the 3-hour 1993 German documentary on the director's life and career, released under its English title *The Wonderful, Horrible Life of Leni Riefenstahl*. The segment of the film dealing with *Triumph of the Will* is especially fascinating, since the interviewer is himself making a documentary and Riefenstahl is explaining her challenges and solutions to a fellow artist. However, it is eerie to watch the look of fascination steal over Riefenstahl's 90-year-old face as she exults in her artistic statement from many years earlier.

# La bataille d'Alger (The Battle of Algiers)

## Film Data

Year: 1966
Director: Gillo Pontecorvo
Screenplay: Franco Solinas
Music: Ennio Morricone
Length: 121 minutes
Rating: No rating

## Connection to *Patterns of World History* & *Patterns of World History, Brief Edition*

Chapter 29: *Reconstruction, Cold War, and Decolonization*

## Preview

The simple musical tune of *The Battle of Algiers* has resonated throughout Western and global society for the past several decades, and the film is justifiably considered one of the most compelling and profound cinematic statements of the twentieth century. Pontecorvo's masterpiece was filmed in Algeria after the outcome of its struggle for independence from France had been determined, and it was inspired by the memoirs of an FLN (National Liberation Front) commander, who appears in the film as a lead character. However, the main setting of the film is in 1956–1957, chronicling a wave of assassinations of police officers in Algiers, bombings and reprisals in both the European quarter and the Casbah, and the French suppression of a general strike in the city. The achievement of the film is unmatched in its combination of the techniques of a documentarian and a cinematic storyteller.

Pontecorvo came to maturity in Fascist Italy, but, due to the imposition of the virulently anti-Semitic race laws in 1938 and afterward, he was unable to secure a university education. Moving to France as a tennis champion, he met several cultural giants like

Picasso, Stravinsky, and Jean-Paul Sartre and heroic veterans of the Spanish Civil War. When war broke out, Pontecorvo returned to Italy and was the leader of Communist youth in anti-Fascist resistance. Many of his films reflect the experience of fighting for freedom, as a proud and determined man of the left, and yet they also reveal the human cost of total commitment to a righteous cause. He has continued to revisit the themes of resistance and collaboration, in a host of contexts and periods, even in his many unfinished or abandoned projects, but his reputation was made in *The Battle of Algiers* and his perspective on violence and terrorism in a Middle Eastern country is as incisive as ever.

In terms of filmmaking, Pontecorvo followed the radical strategy of casting amateurs for nearly all the main parts. He was more concerned, he noted, to employ the right faces, and not to draw on the talents of professional actors. The grainy film style was also deliberate, giving the impression of absolute realism and a documentary feel to the piece. But perhaps the most amazing elements of the film are its musical cues, composed and arranged by Pontecorvo's friend Ennio Morricone. A short tune is repeated in various registers, sometimes softly and sometimes building to a crescendo, and, in a brilliant stroke, a Bach theme plays over the scenes of devastation in a bombed Arab building and reappears over the scenes of bombed sites in the European quarter. Visually, musically, and literally, the people of the world are the same, and every death matters, regardless of the justice of its cause.

## Recommended Scenes

➢ The film opens with a searing scene of an interrogation by torture, between 00:01:33 and 00:09:54. A weeping and shaking man reveals the location of Ali La Pointe's hideout to the French military, and a raid discovers four people, three adults and a child, hiding behind a wall. The scene dissolves into Ali La Pointe's memories since 1954, when he began his association with the FLN and the Algerian resistance generally. Accounting for the sources of Ali's rage, the film shows him being tripped by and then punching a French man, and a list of his 'crimes' against the French occupiers is read out.

➢ The FLN has created a culture of resistance and is already regulating the lives of Algerians, presiding over marriages and harassing drunks and drug abusers in their community, 00:22:18 through 00:27:08. In a series of coordinated attacks, they assassinate police officers and seize their weapons.

➢ Bodies of women and children are picked out of the smoking ruins of a bombed-out building in the Arab quarter, to the strains of a beautiful Bach chamber piece, 00:38:00 through 00:41:40.

➢ The tension-filled and mesmerizing highlight of the film involves the bombing of three French sites, a café, a bar, and an Air France office, with the agency of three women carrying bags, 00:47:16 through 00:57:55. The most remarkable element in this brilliant sequence involves one of the bombers glancing around the café at the people, men, women, and children, who are about to be blown up in the explosion. The French military is called in, and a biography of their commander, Philippe Mathieu, is given. Mathieu had been, ironically, a brave fighter in the Free French resistance to Nazi occupation during the War.

➢ A general strike begins, and Mathieu answers reporters' questions about his plans and tactics, 01:12:45 through 01:14:22. In the meantime, Mathieu is supervising the torture of members of the FLN network, hoping to obtain information about the higher echelons.

➢ A boy grabs a microphone and encourages the strikers, prompting an ululation of support from the women in the Casbah, 01:16:17 through 01:20:58.

➢ Scenes of torture are set to organ music, and Mathieu justifies his tactics in the name of national security and public order, 01:33:10 through 01:38:52.

➢ The scene reverts to the beginning of the film, with the four people in hiding behind a wall. The French attach explosives to the wall and prepare to blow it up. The bombs detonate, and the film ends with descriptions of the eventual independence of Algeria and a woman dancing in jubilation at that point, 01:49:02 through 02:00:40.

## Discussion Questions

1.    How does the film underscore the similarity of people in the European quarter of Algiers and in the Casbah?

2.    How does the film specifically compare Ali La Pointe and Philippe Mathieu?

3.    Does *The Battle of Algiers* justify terrorism?

## Further Reading and Viewing

The three-disc Criterion Collection version of this film, released in 2004, is essential viewing. It contains a series of documentaries, many of them made in the wake of 9/11 and the invasion of Iraq, drawing illuminating and controversial parallels between past and present.

# *Network*

## Film Data

Year: 1976
Director: Sidney Lumet
Created by: Paddy Chayefsky
Length: 121 minutes
Rating: R

## Connection to *Patterns of World History* & *Patterns of World History, Brief Edition*

Chapter 30: *The End of the Cold War, Western Social Transformation, and the Developing World*

## Preview

The presence of television in our lives is so ubiquitous and so commonplace that we cannot fully appreciate how radically this technology has transformed world civilization. Throughout its history, television has competed with the cinema for attention, but the best investigation of television and its power to alter human thought and culture can be found in the 1976 film *Network*.

This sardonic film was the brainchild of Paddy Chayefsky, who had worked for many years in the television industry and had begun work on a screenplay about television news programs in the early 1970s. Specifically reacting to the potential takeover of the ABC network by a worldwide corporation, Chayefsky realized that a profit-driven corporation would probably be unwilling to carry an unprofitable division, as television news had always been. Predicting the future in an uncanny way, he understood that news would have to become an entertainment proposition, driven to ever-more-shocking presentations in order to secure ratings and, thereby, commercial revenue.

The film also predicts the advent of globalization, reality television shows, and our contemporary entertainment culture. As such, it is perhaps even more a document for our time than it was in the 1970s. In an appearance on the Dinah Shore show shortly after the film's release, Chayefsky denied that he had a 'reformist' agenda in composing the screenplay. He commented that his central question was, 'When do we say human life is more important than your lousy dollar?', and he went on to speculate that one day there would be televised gladiatorial games, something on the order of 'Colosseum '77'.

Chayefsky was aided in realizing his vision by the director Sidney Lumet, with whom he had worked at CBS television, and by a circle of perfectly cast actors in both the major and the minor roles. Despite being British, Peter Finch indelibly impersonated an American 'mad prophet of the airwaves', and Faye Dunaway was utterly convincing as the callous embodiment of television itself. Nevertheless, the strongest performances may have been by Ned Beatty, as the prophet of globalization who explains how the world works, and by Beatrice Straight, as a wife who voices all of her emotions as her husband leaves her for another woman. The film deserves to be viewed again and again, and then one should follow Howard Beale's advice and turn off the TV.

## Recommended Scenes

➢ Howard Beale, anchor of the UBS network news program, is fired by his friend and superior Max Schumacher, and together they laugh about the idea of programming a 'suicide of the week', an 'execution of the week', or a 'terrorist of the week'. It still comes as a shock, however, when Beale announces that he will blow his brains out on the air next Tuesday, 00:00:13 through 00:08:01.

➢ At a programming meeting, Diana Christensen develops her idea of creating a television program around an act of real terrorism each week. She declares that the viewing public 'wants someone to articulate their rage'. Howard Beale continues to do this, between 00:13:25 and 00:20:08.

➢ The most famous—and endlessly referenced—scene in the film unspools Beale's 'I'm as mad as hell' speech, between 00:52:21 and 01:01:02. Notice the calm reaction of the station's security guard when Beale comments, 'I must make my witness'.

➢ A revamped Howard Beale show includes a soothsayer and a segment hosted by 'Mata Hari and her Skeletons in the Closet'. Beale begins to tell the truth about television, between 01:02:20 and 01:07:05.

➢ Max falls back into his affair with Diana, and he informs his wife of the relationship in a harrowing scene. A little gem of comedy follows, as a terrorist cell bickers with the network's lawyers over distribution rights and script approval for their program, 01:11:48 through 01:21:28.

➢ When Howard Beale attempts to stop a corporate merger involving UBS, Arthur Jensen delivers a fire-and-brimstone sermon on the glories of capitalism, 01:31:53 through 01:37:45.

➢ UBS executives calmly plan the televised murder of Beale and assess its tie-in value to their other programming. The assassination unfolds, with the commentary that Beale was 'the first known instance of a man being killed because of lousy ratings', 01:53:40 through 01:59:35.

## Discussion Questions

1.    Would a corporate executive be justified in insisting that the news division be profitable?

2.    Is Howard Beale's insistence that 'You've got to get mad!' productive advice?

3.    In 1976, when Arthur Jensen declared, 'Corporations are nations today', was he correct? Would that statement be more accurate today?

## Further Reading and Viewing

For the film's thirtieth anniversary in 2006, a two-disc special edition was released, including an extensive making-of documentary and a remarkable interview with Paddy Chayefsky by Dinah Shore.

# *Entre les murs (The Class)*

## Film Data

Year: 2008
Director: Laurent Cantet
Based on the novel by François Bégaudeau
Length: 130 minutes
Rating: PG-13

## Connection to *Patterns of World History* & *Patterns of World History, Brief Edition*

Chapter 31: *A Fragile Capitalist-Democratic World Order*

## Preview

*Entre les murs* (*Within the Walls* or, in the English version of the title, *The Class*) is a filmed version of François Bégaudeau's experiences as a Parisian schoolteacher. In the course of his teaching, Bégaudeau had encountered a rich—but challenging—mélange of students of various ethnic and religious backgrounds and with various levels of ability and self-discipline. Playing himself in the film, as Monsieur Marin, Bégaudeau drew on his own career and, even more interestingly, interacted with adolescents who were for the most part non-actors and had been encouraged to improvise portions of their performance.

The resulting film poignantly and powerfully conveys the issues and controversies that have arisen in an ostensibly and increasingly multicultural Western Europe. Several nations have been forced to confront their abuses in the colonial period while assimilating, or while resisting the assimilation of, substantial ethnic minorities in their large cities. Simmering frustration and hostility to (at least perceived) racism exploded into a series of riots in Paris' *banlieue* (suburbs) in 2005. Young rioters set cars on fire and were forcibly subdued by the police, and then, in the summer of 2011, a similar spate of violence erupted in London and other British cities in response to the police shooting of a Black teenager.

As so often, the perpetrators and the victims of this sort of violence have been young, and most frequently young men. A school is often the clearest manifestation of a society's aspirations as well as its hatreds, and *The Class* explores these issues through the eyes of an idealistic teacher, but one who is not perfect and makes several errors of judgment. Through his—and the school's—dealings with a single troublesome male student, M. Marin symbolizes some of the difficulties that impede understanding across religious and ethnic lines in today's multicultural Europe. In 2010, German Chancellor Angela Merkel declared, "'*Multikulti' ist tot*', 'Multicultural education and cultural policy is dead'. If this is true, the scene of that death may be 'between the walls' of an urban school.

## Recommended Scenes

➤ A new school year opens in an inner-city Parisian *lycée* (middle to high school), but the teachers are already expressing their doubts and fears for the upcoming term, 00:04:34 through 00:07:48.

➤ A student objects to M. Marin's use of the name 'Bill' in his grammatical examples, and she proposes that he use names like 'Rachid' or 'Ahmed' in its place, 00:12:30 through 00:15:09. As in most of the scenes that concern grammar and proper usage (this is a French class), many of the students feel that they are 'not French' and that their particular cultural experiences are not represented in the dominant culture, symbolized here by their teacher.

➤ After another struggle over 'sequence of tenses', during which students complain that 'no one talks like that anymore, not even my grandmother', one of M. Marin's colleagues briefly breaks down in frustration in the teachers' lounge, 00:26:37 through 00:36:46.

➤ The central story of the film, involving a back-row student called Souleymane, whose family has emigrated from Mali, begins to emerge. M. Marin begins to make tentative steps of progress with him, and Souleymane appears to be reaching out to the concepts M. Marin is introducing, 01:02:43 through 01:12:00.

➤ Souleymane again becomes disruptive in class and is sent to the principal's office, 01:21:40 through 01:23:35.

➤ After a heated exchange in the class among several students, Souleymane flares up in anger, unable to control his hostility, and accidentally injures another student, 01:31:20 through 01:42:20.

➤ A disciplinary hearing is held concerning the matter of Souleymane, after which the boy is expelled from the school and will be sent to another (or, perhaps, to his family's home in Mali). The students are asked what they have learned this year, and one of the girls speaks about Plato's *Republic* and what she has learned from reading about Socrates. A football match seems to hint at a better future for the remaining students in the class, between 01:50:50 and 02:07:02.

## Discussion Questions

1.    How do discussions of grammar result in discussions of racism in French society?

2.    What does the discussion of the assigned reading, *The Diary of Anne Frank*, reveal?

3.    What makes the experiences of Wei, the Chinese student who is in danger of being deported, different from those of Souleymane?

## Further Reading and Viewing

Perhaps the best avenue would be to reflect on one's own experience in high school, and what messages were conveyed by the teachers and the design of the institution as a whole?